RECONFIGURING SOMALI NATION
Changing Conversations, Shifting Paradigms

Adonis & Abbey Publishers Ltd

St James House
13 Kensington Square,
London, W8 5HD
United Kingdom

Website: http://www.adonis-abbey.com
E-mail Address: info@adonis-abbey.com

Nigeria:
Suites C4 – C6 J-Plus Plaza
Asokoro, Abuja, Nigeria
Tel: +234 (0) 7058078841/08052035034

Copyright 2019 © Abdirachid M. Ismail

British Library Cataloguing-in-Publication Data
A catalogue record for this book is available from the British Library

ISBN: 978-1-906704-91-9

The moral right of the author has been asserted

All rights reserved. No part of this book may be reproduced, stored in a retrieval system or transmitted at any time or by any means without the prior permission of the publisher

RECONFIGURING SOMALI NATION
Changing Conversations, Shifting Paradigms

Abdirachid M. Ismail

Acknowledgement

I wish to express my profound gratitude to Prof. Ali Jimale Ahmed who has read the first draft of this work and, from then on, has continuously inspired and encouraged me with his sound and soft thoughts and suggestions. My deep and sincere thanks to Suzanne Lilius who has put so much time and effort to proofread the book and has enlightened me with her knowledge about the Somali-Issa political organisation. I am also tremendously appreciative to the reviewers, Dr. Abdi M. Kusow, Dr. Amina S. Chiré, Dr. Hamdi Mohamed, Fowsia Abdulkadir and Zaynab A. Sharci, who has generously contributed to this work with their comments and critics.

I would like to extend my thanks to my dear wife, Maryam Ali Ahmed, who always accompanies me in my intellectual adventures and often takes the lion's share in the most thankless, but essential, parts of my works before the finalization of these. My warm thanks also to my dear brother Idan Benoit Frumence who has actively and cheerfully facilitated the publishing of this book, and to Hibo Mohamed Youssouf who has used her wonderful skills as a photographer and designer to produce the cover of it.

Finally, i would like to thank heartfully all my friends and colleagues of the Independent Research Institute of the Horn of Africa **(IRICA)** who, through volunteer work and little means, carry the burden to promote the scientific research in Djibouti, especially. I cannot end this acknowledgement without expressing our deep indebtedness to Moussa Ali Meigague, the Director of the Institute of Diplomatic Studies of Djibouti who endlessly gives support to IRICA, simply because he understands deeply the importance of scientific research for global development and the necessity to share its results with general public.

Table of Contents

Acknowledgment iv

General Introduction vi

Chapter One
New Insights on Culture: The E³ Theory 11
   1. Introduction 11
   2. Basic Assumptions 15
   3. Culture Variation 35
   4. Towards a Culture of Spirit 40
   5. Conclusion 41
References: Chapter I 43

Chapter Two
Cultural Dimension in State Building: Focus on Somali Case 47
Part I- The Past as a Mirror 47
   1. Introduction 47
   2. Somalia Central State Collapse: Diagnosis 52
   3. Inexorable Events towards SUPP Failure 72
   4. Conclusion 77
References: Chapter II- Part 1 78

Part II- The Future in the Present 87
   1. The New Project 87
   2. General Conclusion 107
References: Chapter II- Part 2 111

Book Review 117

Index 135

General Introduction

In 2011, I met for the first time a Somali child whose parents had decided to make him a *dhaqan celis*, literally, "return to culture", which refers to the fact that Somali parents from the international diaspora sometimes send their children back home for different reasons which we will see below. This twelve-year-old child was born in Netherlands, from Somali parents. He had shown serious behavioural problems according to his entourage (disobedience, anger, opposition, provocation, etc.) at home and at school. This led the school director to summon his parents one day after a major crisis that led to the intervention of the police, to tell them that they could no longer keep their child in the school and that he needed to be brought into a specialized institution.

Marja Tilikaninen (2011)[1] mentions different reasons which justify this *dhaqan celis* among Somalis. She says that it takes place because "they [the kids submitted to *dhaqan celis*] have committed crimes, become mentally ill, abused drugs or otherwise adopted lifestyles that contradict their parents' or custodians' understanding of decent behaviour". The child in question here is definitely related to the last case.

I was introduced to him in Djibouti, a few weeks after his arrival in this country, in a restaurant. While his father was telling me why he had brought his son back to the country, while the rest of his family had remained in Europe, the young boy who was playing in the area came to his father. The later wanted to introduce him to me and after extending my hand and exchanging a few words, he sat down beside me. At the second that followed, he took the hat that I had on my head, to put it on his own. His father reprimanded him and ordered him to put the hat back in its place. Naturally, he did not, but his elbows resting on the table and holding his chin with both hands, he wore a broad smile. Looking at him with the same smile and passing my hand on my head, I explained to him that he had hair and that I had none and that consequently I needed this hat more than him. His smile widened and he put back the hat on my head carefully.

---

[1] Marja Tilikainen, 2011, "Failed Diaspora: Experiences of *Dhaqan Celis* and Mentally Ill Returnees in Somaliland", Nordic Journal of African Studies 20(1): 71–89.

After this gesture, I exchanged a few words with him, about his old and his new life and his answers seemed quite coherent. But very quickly, he rose from the table to go around the restaurant. I saw him two or three times later and at each time I was told by his father or grand-father or by any other person of his family, the "nonsense" he had done lately, such as smoking a butt, arguing with passersby, wandering for hours outside the house, leaving for adventure by taking a bus at random and so on. It was not easy to "hold" him.

Being neither a psychologist nor a paediatrician, it was difficult for me to describe this type of behaviour, but this child reminded me a lot about those children who are called in Somali *qalqaali*, that is to say "restless, uncontrollable, turbulent". That's all! One could find him alive, enterprising, too extroverted and dispelled. He did not understand the authority of parents and elders and required extremely important attention, which is not always easy for single parents, who work and have many children. Culture, education and psychology are interwoven in the case of this child...but what this means exactly? Are these notions truly disconnected?

This case had awakened in me the issue of culture, in relation to the traditional education that we could receive in our African countries. But *dhaqan celis* is not only about children who may have, as in the case mentioned earlier, attitudes which could be considered to be outside of what is perceived as the rule in terms of behaviour and social relations. It may simply concern a youth who is not "fluent in the Somali language and is dressed differently from local youths" (Marja Tilikainen, *id.*, p.77).

I thought of these young people, whose parents migrated to the western countries to improve their living conditions and who were torn apart (socially and psychologically) between two or more cultures, between two or more worlds. Fortunately, the majority of these kids manage somehow to develop a sort of median, semi-official culture, marginalized by some and decried by others, until they find the dominant cultural trend of the place where they live.

While the centrality of the question of culture in the evolution of human life appeared to me day by day, I fell "by chance" on the work of Richard Dawkins[2] (1976, 2006), *Selfish Gene,* which opened to me a whole

---

[2] Richard Dawkins, 2006, *Selfish Gene*, OUP Oxford, edited firstly in 1976.

literature relating to a field quite new to me, *sociobiology*. The work of Charles Lumsden and Edward Wilson (1981, 2006)[3], *Gene, Mind and Culture*, have come to reinforce an unformulated idea of culture far from the socio-anthropological conception in which this notion is locked up in the mind of the general public and is somewhat the basement and the outcome of *The Clash of Civilizations*[4].

Beyond the *dhaqan celis* practice amongst Somali diaspora, there is another phenomena related to culture which has motivated this book. Today's world is governed by two seemingly opposing trends which have seemingly motivated the clash mentioned earlier: namely an integrative and centripetal force, stimulated by communication technologies and the development of exchanges, and a centrifugal force stimulated by psycho-sociological representations and the desire to maintain identities and particularities. The global invades more and more the local, which resists or agrees to participate in this globalization of human affairs and virtualization of state borders. These two trends are powerful, each driven by extreme motivations, on the one hand the economic imperatives and policies that push people to exchange and get closer and not to make war and on the other, the fear of getting lost into the other and the unknown. On the one hand, there is an immense need to open up and shatter all forms of frontiers, on the other hand, the need, no less powerful, to situate oneself, to identify oneself and to connect oneself to a history.

In addition, the economic imbalances between countries and within countries causing waves of migration, the emergence of new economically competitive nations, the renewal of ideological struggles, between global currents and regional currents, between secular currents and religious movements, all this raises tensions and questions. At the border of these tendencies, forces or currents is situated the element of culture. And a new understanding of what culture ultimately is could open up a path for 21st century humanity to move less noisily toward its destiny. At least that's what we hope for through this little contribution on culture.

---

[3] Charles Lumsden and Edward Wilson, 2006, *Gene, Mind and Culture*, World Scientific Publishing Co., New York; 1st edited in 1981.
[4] Samuel Huntington, 1997, *Le choc des civilisations*. Odile Jacob.

This book proposed here, is thus, composed of two parts which seem independent, but, whose contents highlight each other. The first is devoted to the theoretical reflection of culture in relation to the issues raised above. The second part is a review of the recent history of Somalia and the Somali nation through this understanding of culture, established in the first part.

CHAPTER ONE

New Insights on Culture: The E³ Theory

1. Introduction

Culture is considered in different ways by anthropologists. Some consider it a catalogue of traits, such as beliefs, knowledge, technics, arts, etc., which characterize and encompass a person or a society. Some others give more importance to the process of acquiring these characteristics or traits. These include Radcliffe-Brown (1952: 4–5[1]) who defines culture as:

> ...the process by which a person acquires, from contact with other persons or from such things as books or works of art, knowledge, skill, ideas, beliefs, tastes, sentiments". Still others such as Robert Redfield relate culture "to the way of doing, thinking, feeling[2].

In 1871, Edward Burnett Tylor gave his well-known and now most-quoted definition of culture in his work *Primitive Culture*. According to him, "[Culture] is that complex whole which includes knowledge, beliefs, arts, morals, laws, customsand any other capability and habits acquired by [a human] as a member of society."[3]

Though this definition has been elaborately discussed and refuted by many scholars (Kroeber and Kluckhohn, 1952), it still remains relevant, causing UNESCO to refer to it as the common definition[4], and Spencer & Aout (2012) as being the "foundational definition for anthropology". Does this mean that almost one and half century of continuous effort has not thrown up how to formulate a common theory to explain the different aspects of this concept? Or is it because, as L. Lowell wrote in 1915[5], "there is nothing in the world more elusive than culture", and that "one cannot define or circumscribe it", since "it has no precise bounds"? Is culture like the elephant in the dark house described by blind people?

Kroeber and Kluckhohn (1952) provided about three hundred definitions of culture in their book and came to the synthetic conclusion that "culture consists of patterns, explicit and implicit, of and for behaviour acquired and transmitted by symbols, constituting the distinctive achievement of human groups, including their embodiments in artefacts; the essential core of culture consists of traditional (i.e., historically derived and selected) ideas and especially their attached values; culture systems may, on the one hand, be considered as products of action, on the other as conditioning elements forfurther action (1952:181)[6]".

This definition contains the basic notions of the different conceptions about culture, but fails to reveal the interrelations between these notions. White, reviewing Kroeber and Kluckhohn's work, opines that the book, even with the attempt at providing a compendium of definitions of culture, has not provided any clarification about what culture is. "I believe that confusion has increased as conceptions of culture have been multiplied and diversified" White (1959)[7]. In fact, speaking about system or systems without discussing the relationships between the elements of any such specific system, is like describing a tree as being made of branches, leaves, flowers and fruits without perceiving the unity of all these elements.

The question, then, is how to reconcile all theseconceptions of culture. How to reconcile the diverse approaches employed in Anthropology, Sociology, Psychology or Biology, without running a risk of a blissful but inconsistent syncretism? To answer this question, it is necessary to go back to the fundamental structure of culture, to delve into its atomic structure and determine its elementary components. From such a vantage point, it is possible to find consistent and common points in all the conceptions and definitions of culture.

Background

Even though the notion of culture is so common and significant for each of us, it is nevertheless difficult to delimit and define it. It has become trivial, even among anthropologists, to consider it as being everything. Number of disciplines, from Philosophy to Anthropology, through

Sociology, Psychology and even Biology and Ethology have approached the term in so many different ways. The result of that recalls the metaphor of the elephant in a dark room described by blind people. Whatever one says, the description will always be partial, because everyone has access to a part of the cultural puzzle.

However, it was noticed that the different conceptions of culture, rather than the contradiction of each other, are used to describe the different levels of culture corresponding to different levels of life development. For an instance, the elitist approach which has dominated the Nineteenth Century (cf. Matthew Arnold, 1867) and had its principal support from the *Evolution of Species theory*, refers to the highest level of human development as the scholars used to perceive it at that time. They base their assumptions on the analogy with the agricultural field which the word "culture" derives etymologically and refers to the "development of intellectual faculties of man opposed to what he would have if he stays in his natural state". Indeed, "natural state" refers to a person who is barren of intellectual work, like a field which is not laboured. This elitist meaning still exists nowadays and even has strong support from contemporary intellectuals[8] opposed to cultural relativism and mass consumerism.

In the first part of the last century, structural anthropology developed by Franz Boas[9], Edward Sapir[10], Claude Lévi-Strauss[11], etc. introduced another view which emphasises on the relativism in the hierarchy of cultures defended by elitists and evolutionists such as Arnold, Spencer, Taylor or Morgan, the latter believing that culture proceeds from "savagery" to "civilization" passing through "barbarism". With the development of ethology on the one hand and molecular biology on the other, a wider perspective of culture comes up.

What are the common points of all these conceptions? If culture is to be approached as a scientific object, new insights are needed to formulate a synthetic idea about the main theories or conceptions. Having considered the foundations of various theories, from that of Matthew Arnold (1867), to that of the Neo-Darwinist ethologists and biologists of the second half of the last century postulating a parallelism between biological evolution and the evolution of culture (Richard Dawkins, 1976, 2006, Dennett 1995, Blakemore 1999), we will endeavor to identify the essential contribution of each approach, before presenting the hypothesis whichwill be explained and lent credence in this book and which could differentiatethe source of culture, its structure, its operation and its aim.

Evolution of Conceptions

After the elitist approach, the cultural relativism which goes back at least to the writings of Johann von Herder, if we set aside the ancient Greeks such as Herodotus or Protagoras and their ideas about relativity of human views and beliefs, dominates the anthropological approaches almost since the beginning of the Twentieth Century. Even if after the development of genetics and molecular biology, the neo-Darwinians, with their renewed evolutionist theory and attempt to build a Global theory of Evolution,12 impacted the conception about culture, the structural theory has remained the main reference. And Tylor's definition, in spite of its evolutionist underlying principle, satisfies somewhat the structuralist view since he defines culture as a "complex whole", in other words, as a system of symbols rooted in a specific ecological setting. Every culture has a unity in its different parts (beliefs, artefacts, arts, way of life, etc.) relevant with each other and with its environment.

It is commonplace to say that theories are not independent of the social and ideological context from which they emerged. The elitist and evolutionist theories are deep rooted in the aristocratic and bourgeois societies, before the 19th centuryand the evolutionists after Darwin's Origin of Species and the colonization period which revealed more strongly the western ethnocentrism which had been denounced already by the philosophy of the enlighteners. The cultural relativism will have more impact in the second half of the 20th century which questioned the supposed superiority of western civilisation after the barbarism of Nazism and Fascism.

The end of the last century which has experienced a tremendous development of genetics has brought up to date the application of Darwinian theory into culture. The success of Richard Dawkins's *Selfish*

Gene, in the wake of genetics, computer development and artificial intelligence, illustrates the resurgence of this conception.

But it seems to us that this approach is not merely a resurgence of the evolutionary theory of the 40-50s, which is in fact a continuation of the elitist and ethnocentric theory for which Darwinism was thought to be a sound scientific justification. In fact, for the first time, there is an attempt to reveal culture in its substance and not in its manifestations. It is not only to describe cultures as coherently constitutedbodies, but to reveal the elementary composition which permits these bodies to come up. But before doing this, it is necessary to establish the basic assumptions on which the theory, which has been developed here, is based on.

2. Basic Assumptions

These assumptions are:
- Culture is in fact what permits human beings to achieve a better knowledge and rise above one's condition to access a higher state of being.
- Culture is formed of some precise units which function as a cohesive,interactive and dynamic system
- Culture changes in space and time, to adjust itself to its ecological setting
- Culture is an outcome of human global evolution. It is the last offspring of the process of biological evolution.

Culture : The Modus Operandi of Human Resilience

Resilience comes originally from Physics and illustrates the ability of a material to return to its original shape after having been submitted to a physical force which has bent or distorted it. In psychology it has been used since the beginning of 70's[13] to describe the capacity of a person has to recover from a trauma, to face misfortune and stressed situations or simply to cope with change. In human sciences (Sociology, Economy, Anthropology, etc.), resilience can be summed as having enough capacity in terms of economic resources, moral strength and technical ability to face a difficult situation, a misfortune caused by environmental catastrophe or a sudden change of one's own environment.

To put in relation the physicists' definition with this broad human sciences view, resilience can be seen as the capacity of an entity to absorb, first, a loss of energy and then to compensate it and get back to its original state. This entity can be a material, an institution, a community or a living being. One thing which distinguishes all these entities is the nature as well as the degree of their resilience. The material items have an intrinsic natural resilience, while human beings construct much of their resilience individually or collectively. We assume that the construction of this resilience is what we call culture.

It is trite to say that culture is rooted in an environment. Environment is the first constraint to any human being since from the beginning it does not satisfy all his needs (physical, psychological and spiritual). The human being will then embark on a venture of acquisition of knowledge to face the environmental obstacles in the forms of biological, physical or social obstacles.

Freud's definition of Kultur[14] is linked to this idea. He writes:

> The word 'civilization' [Kultur] describes the whole sum of the achievements and regulations which distinguish our lives from those of our animal ancestors and which serve two purposes - namely to protect men against nature and to adjust their mutual relations[15] (1930, p. 89).

This view recalls the conception based on the dichotomy established by many authors between nature and culture which will end with Morgan's hierarchy, as far as human societies are concerned. If we follow Freud in his conception, Culture can then be viewed as what enables mankind to be resilient.

It is easy to understand how economic resources, social organizations, agricultural techniques and even morality can relate to resilience. But literature, philosophy, art, architecture or aesthetics in general, how can they be related to resilience?

This relation is perceived by Malinowski (1944) who went further by connecting them with basic needs: "economics, knowledge, religion and mechanisms of law, educational training and artistic creativeness are directly or indirectly related to the basic, that is, physiological needs[16]" (p. 120). He defines these elementary or basic needs "as the environmental and biological conditions which must be fulfilled for the survival of the individual and the group" (p. 75). He thus counts a number of physiological needs (breathing, sleep, rest, nutrition, excretion and reproduction) which express themselves as a tension on the body and which must be satisfied, otherwise, the survival of the individual or the group is not guaranteed. These needs are linked to the "Biological determinism which forces upon human behavior certain invariable sequences, which must be incorporated into every culture, however refined or primitive, complex or simple" (p. 79). Thus, the concept of "culture" is related to that of "resilience", itself linked to that of "need" since, as Malinowski (id., p.75-76) writes "the concept of need is merely the first approach to the understanding of organized human behavior." From this perspective, Malinowski's definition (p.36) of culture is consistent when he says:

> It obviously is the integral whole consisting of implements and consumers' goods, of constitutional charters for the various social groupings, of human ideas and crafts, beliefs and customs. Whether we consider a very simple or primitive culture or an extremely complex and developed one, we are confronted by a vast apparatus, partly material, partly spiritual, by which man is able to cope, with the concrete, specific problems which confront him[17.]

So, in short, culture is this "integral whole...partly material, partly spiritual" which enables humans to cope with the specific problems they are confronted with.

Art, which expresses ideas and feelings about existence and tend to socialize and humanize mankind, is also a powerful tool to infuse good, beauty, truth and wonder, according to Kant[18]. This Kantian conception is the classical view on which is based the opposition between nature and culture, the art being considered as this part of human creativity which enables individuals to train their minds and sensitivity to obtainan independent judgement, opposed to "popular cultures" (cf. Finkerkraut, *La défaite de la pensée*, 1987).

To sum up, culture is an « integrated whole" which permits Mankind to cope with the obstacles and difficulties of its environment. In other words, culture is what makes human beings resilient. From that perspective, we can thus imagine the consequences when allogenic cultural traits are infused in another culture, the impact it can have in the society and individuals in terms of resilience. At best, this society will experience cultural and societal disturbances, in adapting to these and integrating these elements, at worst it will progressively weaken this society enough to make it subject to an exogenous cultural domination or a cultural shift. This demands a great amount of energy to overcome the crisis which arises usually from this kind of shift, especially if this shift comes up abruptly.

Culture as a Mean to Survive

Malinowski's view of culture has been criticized by Lévi-Strauss as reducing Culture to « an immense metaphor of reproduction and digestion[19]". But it appears that Malinowski and Levy-Strauss are considering two different levels of culture which are illustrated below.

The assumption which has been discussed and defended in this paper is that in the very beginning of Man's existence, Culture had been more likely about what Malinowski describes, a mean to survive, than that of Kantian conception based on what we call today "high culture". And even more, culture can be seen as the last phase of biological development as defended by neo-Darwinists like Edward Wilson (1975), Charles Lumsden and Edward Wilson (1981, 2006) and described at length by Dawkins's in his Selfish Gene. This late author (Dawkins, 1976, 2006) who is, as far I know, one of those scholars who applied Darwin's theory to human nature to the last consequences, presents culture as being the result of evolution of genes which gave rise to new replicators called the "memes[20]". These memes were not constituted by chemical molecules, but by "…tunes, ideas, catch-phrases, clothes fashions, ways of making pots or of building arches" (Dawkins, 2006:192) and by all that which we usually call cultural traits such as beliefs, food, games, sex roles, etc.

This idea forces us to review our conception of culture which is often considered only in its latest phases, as a symbolic system transmitted through generations. Whereas, an idea, a symbol, or whatever "meme" which could be transmitted, needs first to be created. And what creates the meme? Malinowski answers "physiological needs", and Dawkins, "genetic evolution", both meaning the necessity of life.

Following these authors, culture is first a mean to survive. Dawkins stipulates that, after the long reign of gene survival policy, culture through the memes has inherited the power to run the survival of the human species, even if they are still subservient to the general policy of their "master programmers[21]". He says "We are built as gene machines and cultured as meme machines" (*id.*, p.201).

Memes' high degree of survival, as genes, is based on "longevity, fecundity and copying-fidelity". Longevity, depending on the number of "copies" the meme goes through, fecundity, its speed of reduplication, and copying-fidelity, achieves the capacity to remain stable during transmission. So, culture is a system of memes which, like genes, transmit themselves through the process of natural selection: "But just as not all genes that can replicate do so successfully, some memes are more successful in the meme-pool than others. This is the analogue of natural selection." (Dawkins, *id.*, p.194).

Dawkins's vision about the development of memes describes in fact what things are, when we consider especially human technics of production: a production technique appears, it spreads and is transmitted from generation to generation until a more effective technic replaces the functions of it. But all human cultural products are not about production and the authors give rational explanations about how a meme-idea or a tune or some more abstract memes followthe same process of evolution.

We have understood so far that culture is a system of things which makes Mankind resilient and helps it to survive. We have accepted Dawkins's statement which describes these things as memes, some kind of macro-genes[22] produced by genes themselves and thus functioning according to the same pattern, meaning natural selection.

Before going deeper into the level of molecules, we need to stay at the human level to understand what these things are made of and how they constitute a system.

Culture as a Process of Attaining a Better State of Being

This is somewhat one of the most ancient definitions of the word « culture » which refers to the development of one's mind through appropriate exercises. This meaning will lead to the birth of formal education. It is the last part of the cultural process which we are aware of until now. But underlying this part, there is a primitive and unconscious part which has been growing since the being has come to existence and has given birth to what we call "culture". This first pedestal part has taken place in the microscopic level of the being and has followed the Darwinian biological evolution. There is no gap between the two as Richard Dawkins states in his Selfish Gene, in which he illustrates how genes gave rise to memes, the name given to culture's fundamental unitof organisation.

To understand how we can move from genes to memes, we need to start from the basic constituents of human culture.

Basic Constituents of Human Culture

As in Tylor's definition, in all definitions of culture, whatever the discipline they are rooted in, Anthropology, Sociology, Psychology, Genetics or Ethology, they share two common and minimum elements which are information and transmission. To these two basic elements we add environment, in its wider meaning of physical, biologicaland social setting. One can stress on one aspect or the other, replacing one term by another, (i.e information by knowledge, environment by society, transmission by sharing or acquiring something, etc.), the fact is that culture means that something is learnt and is transmitted to another generation of living beings, for their benefit. This idea is clearly expressed by Matsumoto (1996:16)[23] who sees culture as "the set of attitudes, values, beliefs and behaviors shared by a group of people, but different for each individual, communicated from one generation to the next.[24]"

It has become commonplace to say that animals transmit also learnt information to younger generation[25], and as such, possess something that many ethologists have labeled as "culture". In fact, their works and reports showed that during the second half of last century these three elements mentioned above are shared with animals such as primates, cetacean, honey bees, etc. (*cf.* Matsuzawan 2006[26]; Bonner, John Tyler, 1980[27] ;Rendell L. and H. Whitehead, 2001[28], etc.) and for this reason, speak very rightly about "animal culture". This contributes strongly to the biological evolutionist's arguments which apply Darwinian theory to human behaviours.

What should be said now is that, whereas these three core elements, environment, information and transmission, shared by human beings and animals, we have the basic foundation of what we call "culture". This can recall the Edgard Morin vision of the 'principe trialectique[29]" who considers that the most primitive form of the universe is made of Matter-Information and Energy. But it is now necessary to dig further into these three elements to grasp what they refer to more precisely and in what extent humans and animals differentiate themselves from each other.

i)   Environment

Environment can be a physical location, since geography influences culture. People surrounded by sea are more likely to develop a fishing culture than those who live in the Sahara. Environment is also social, according to the type of society (hunting and gathering, pastoral, agricultural, industrial, etc.), some types of cultural features will be found related to family sizes, sex relationships, leaderships or governance, etc.

At the human, animal or plant levels, we can speak of geography or space, but at the microscopic level, the term "environment" takes a different meaning, which is that of ecologyor the broader meaning of "medium". A cell also lives in a medium which is that of the organ to which it belongs to but is individualized within a plasma envelope among the other cells. At a smaller level, the cell nucleus is found in a medium (that of the cytoplasm) protected by the nuclear membrane of the nucleus, surrounded by multitudes of organelles (Ribosomes, Mitochondria, Peroxisome, Microtubule, etc.) And more deeply, the chromatid appears in the nucleoplasmic medium of the nucleus, which is separated from the organelles by a nuclear envelope. Inside the chromatid one the nucleolus could be found inside which RNA and DNA molecules are found, as well as other types of proteins such as enzymes. At each level, there is a change of environment, although these environments are interdependent and are all organized with the aim of a higher evolution. But each medium is organized around a nucleus, a head which governs the other elements connected to it from multiple directions.

If we consider the macroscopic levels, the being is also connected to a set of "environments", regarding the stellar level (the influence of the solar or zodiacal system), planetary (or atmospheric), geographical, social and relational. Each medium is a system with rules of its own, the aim of which always is the same: to maintain harmony between the various elements that compose it in order to allow the emergence or the existence of a higher level of organization. If harmony is not maintained, the life system is compromised as well as its subsequent evolution.

If we take homo sapiens-sapiens, it has gone through an internal and external evolution to reach a state of understanding of the different environments in which it could find itself (psychic, physical and social) in order to know the importance of establishing an organized society. The broader the consciousness and the understanding of life, the wider and more complex the system in which the interation takes place. From the family, we move on to society and the political territory, then to supra-territorial organizations, such as empires and world organizations. Indeed this movement throughout these different phases is not linear and uniform; it depends on the type of ecology in which individuals live (in terms of external pressure, availability of resources, degree of homogeneity of the members, geographical configuration, etc.)

In any case, life is inscribed in different layers of "environments" (space or medium) which balance conditions which are necessary for the development for life. The rules and laws that govern this balance and harmony at the cellular level are mechanical and unconscious since they are beyond the perception and free will of human being. At the societal level, man realizes the necessity of this balance and harmony in order to continue to live; it is why he consciously institutes the rules and laws that allow him to achieve this goal. It is that process that we call "culture", in the institutional sense. In fact, this process is a continuous progress which emerges from the "mechanical" level of development of life to that "institutionalized" development of human deeds and productions. This recalls the elitist definition of culture, highlighting the progress from "the state of nature to that of a higher state of being".

The different layers in which the living entity develops itself (not to speak of matter) are interlinked, although these layers are not acting with the same force on this entity which could be related to the considerations from the highest level, namely the galactic level, for which we have not yet a proof of its influence on terrestrial life, up to the cellular level. We can use the common terminology of these different layers or levels, to specify the same, namely the universe (the galactic level), the solar system, the world (global), the environment (local), the medium (social/familial) and the terrain (biological). Since these spaces are interconnected, it is not easy to delineate them truly. The terrain is the scene where the transformation of the entity takes place. This transformation is either induced by the elements of the terrain, themselves influenced by progressive stages of the other layers, but it also can be spontaneous. This spontaneity, which marks a qualitative leap towards a more complex organization, cannot be random, since it seems to be done in the direction of a "greater consciousness".

Thus, what we call "environment" is actually a permeable space, comparable to a Russian doll that is organized in different layers that communicate with one another through different canals. At each level, the living entity is in a state that influences its immediate and distant space, as it is influenced by it. There is no gap between this space (comparable to the "soma" of Weismann[30]) and the living entity (its "germen"). They are linked by means of exchanges more or less tangible. In the cell, there is no closure between the nucleus and the cytoplasm, as in the egg there is no closure between the egg yolk (nucleus) and the egg-white and so, there is no closure between Man and his physical environment, otherwise death would stop the process of evolution. It is why Malinowski (1960:37) says that "environment is neither more nor less than culture itself". It is therefore important to consider these different interlacing and interdependent "environments" that condition the evolution of any living entity.

For the Darwinian evolution theory, soma or space has come before "germen" or life. This is the philosophical postulation of materialistic vision of universe which limits creation to the physical sphere. This part of this theory is neither proven nor capable to explain the high degree of predictability found in the universe. It inevitably leads to the idea of an evolution that happens by chance. The proponents of this hypothesis prefer to simulate ignorance and to pretend that there is no fact which could prove the process of evolution towards a greater state of consciousness, when they have before their eyes the results of millions of years of evolution.

The intelligent design theory which explains that intelligence pre-exists than those of "soma" or space, seem consistent with the rise of culture which is the fruit of this intelligence-germen. This intelligent entity seems to be the alpha and omega of culture, the seed and the fruit. It begins to be wrapped in a space, created by itself and evolves in this space in a more and more complex manner and grows up until it becomes aware of its own intelligence and acts to increase this awareness. This process of increasing awareness or intelligence is fundamentally what we called culture. Space-Soma will be the "it" which could be a part of oneself, which fuels the self, which influences it, but which is not itself in a complete and comprehensive manner.

The first great revolution in the evolution of awareness for the living entity is to disassociate itself from soma, the space that contains it and to assert the specificity of itself, in spite of the intimate intricacy with the material space. This revolution reaches its climax at the stage that Winnicott calls "the delusion of being God" where the child realizes that his mother's womb is not his, but is distinct from himself and that he himself is a singular being. From that moment on, for him/her there will the "I/me", "the thing" and "the other", that is to say, the basic elements of culture. From a Winnicottien view, it can be a previous stage where there is only "I" and "not-me"[31]"

This awareness of the different levels of "open space" during the 20th century, particularly thanks to quantum physicsand the deepening of knowledge in biology (see Ludwig von Bertalanffy and his open systems[32]) drives to think of a new scientific epistemology linking these levels. This is the reason why "recent years have seen the leading thinkers of many fields of scholarly work (including the science of complexity, Ecology, Education, integral studies, Philosophy, Psychology, Spirituality and systems theory) proclaim that the modes of thought of the last century, fragmented, mechanistic and materialistic, are no longer sustainable".[33]

The underlying assumption of what we can call the "open space" theory is based on the fact that the living being is continuously moving from one environment to another: i.e. from the mother womb environment, to that of the nuclear family and to that of a larger social environment and finally to that of national and more global ecosystems. There is the necessity of life, the "life force" which needs continuously to grow and go from one environment to an ever larger and more complex one, to satisfy greater individual pleasures or needs. In other words, when a being becomes mature and fully adapted to one environment, it passes to the higher environment. But it is also confronted with the opposite tendency induced by the self-preservation instinct which considers "openness" as a risk for one's life. It is the dilemma in which the individual is confronted with the compulsion concerning the widening of one's space of interaction to have a more exciting life and weighing it against the risk against one's preservation. Going through a new environment and getting adapted to it requires more energy and this presents the risk of the unknown, the dangers to one's self-preservation.

In one word, environment is made of intricate ecosystems which permit life to achieve effective growth continuously. But for this purpose, the individual needs to learn and capitalize on the experiences received from every phase or cycle of his development.

ii) Education

As has been mentioned above, at the human level, culture was meant to be the process to improve Human intellectual abilities, to elevate him/her from the level of the natural or animalistic behaviour to that more idealistic state called "civilized being". To reach that goal, there is a central concept without which the process cannot be achieved and which could be identified as education. Education is basically described as transmission of a higher knowledge, it is why education is fundamentally based on information.

It is a key concept in the evolution of any dynamic system. For any entity which evolves, the information must circulate between the successive and scalable states of the entity. For that purpose, it should be necessary to have a structure for storing information (memory). In summary, it should at least have three capacities: (A) Capacity to experiment with its environment, (B) Capacity to register and processes experience (information); (C) Capacity to memorize and transmit results of the experimentation. The experimentation of the environment creates knowledge, which is stored and then transmitted.

Culture is often defined as the transmission of a certain measure of knowledge and behaviour, in other words a certain amount of information which could be deemed adequate in a certain "environment". Considering this fact, "cultural transmission is analogous to genetic transmission in that, though basically conservative, it can give rise to a form of evolution", as Dawkins puts it.

As in the levels of the human beings, the cell which is the smallest living entity[34] is equipped with a device that experiences and feeds on its environment, which records and selects its sensations. These sensations are transmitted to the daughter cell which could be born from the mother cell. The analogy established between the cell and the human body is common, when we consider respiration mechanisms, feeding processes, excretion functioning; the cell nucleus acting as the brain, with its role of control and memorization of information.

We have seen that the living entity was circumscribed in a space divided into different levels or interdependent layers. The more the entity is developed, the more its space expands and becomes more complex. This complexity goes hand in hand with the emergence of additional skills which make it capable of taking advantage of its environment (at each level or layer, there is a need for special skills) and to widen its living space, or its chance of survival.

From the automatic transmission of biochemical information to the transmission of knowledge formalized by an educational institution, passing through the transmission of informal knowledge through mimicry, we have here the long development of culture from its primal phase to its human phase.

The debate that shakes up education, about what should be transmitted or not, since the second half of the previous century, is related to the growing mass of knowledge of modern societies and the consecutive change of their needs. For centuries, education (instruction) was seen as a set of knowledge to be transmitted to the child-pupil, so that he could acquire and reproduce the norms of his society, which was often un-democratic and highly elitist. But this approach is seen totally inadequate today because it reduces the opportunity for the child to be prepared to a more complex environment. It was a self-preservation based education and not a life dynamic based education.

From the second half of the Twentieth Century until now, the school is seen less as a place where one acquires only practical knowledge such as reading, writing and counting, than a place that must stimulate and awaken potentialities. The education system opts for a kind of pedagogy that is less directive and more participative, which aims to produce "well-made heads". However, this pedagogy did not have a theoretical and ideological base on the process of culture evolution analysis and thus had terminated at a dead-end. For instance, although culture has to do with the increase of intellectual faculties, as has been stated above, the link with spiritual development had not been seen and has so far been not observable yet. . Instead, academics continue to see the concept of 'spirit' either as an equivalent of intellect or something tainted with irrationality.

The school, without having yet passed this debate, was affected by a sudden change of the environment with the onset of the oil crisis and structural unemployment in western countries. All of the global events such as long-term economic crisis and geopolitical change in the 80's and 90's, with the disappearance of the world ideological bipolarity, followed by the development of new technologies of communication and the beginning of globalization had introduced disparate approaches about education linked to this new unstable environment.

With the new Technologies of Information and Communication (NTIC), there is a new environment in world transactions which introduces undoubtedly a new paradigm for mankind. Electronic information is characterized by its high speed of exchange and implies an increasing speed of action and reaction, speed in thinking and speed in making decisions. Can man be faster than a machine to make a decision? Would man be able to beat a machine in decision making based on quantity of information available? The answer is no. The deep-blue performance in 1997 facing one of the most well-trained human minds is a testimony of this assertion. So how should human beings be trained and educated in this new environment of NTIC? There is again the same question which was asked in the beginning of the 70's and which has not been solved, since education did not permit to avert the different world crises (moral, political, economic, financial, etc.) from the end of the 90's until now.

The assumption asserted the purpose of education and its links with the concept of resilience and the new environment settled by the NTIC, should permit to trace the consistent approach of education for the 21st century.

iii) Experience

Once the information obtained through the experimentation of its environment and is memorized for later use (Atkinson and Shiffrin, 1968)[35], then comes the phase of its transmission to the following generation. This transmission of the experience, received from its environment and validated on the basis of previous "knowledge" acquired during its evolution, is mechanic at the cellular level. It is done through the natural selection of the most efficient options. On human level, it is performed through a more or less organized process, through the social institutions (family, school, media, etc.) as it appears in Malinowski's assertion:

It is clear that, as culture advances, the various occupational and specific functional tasks become gradually differentiated and incorporated into specific institutions. As education must exist amongst the lowest primitives (indeed, as the transmission of traditional techniques, values and ideas) then, it must have existed from the very beginning of humanity. But it is incorporated into the family, the local group, the association of playmates, the age-grade and the economic guild of craftsmen where the novice receives his apprenticeship. Special institutions for the training of the young such as the schools, colleges and universities, are some of the newest acquisitions of humanity. In the same way true knowledge and indeed, science, were present at the earliest stages of culture.

At the cellular level, the experiment results from recordings of biochemical reactions that take place inside the cell and transmitting them to the daughter cells. It is not necessary for us to go into details here, the important thing for us to notice has been the passage during the biological evolution of a mechanical and unconscious transmission of the experience to a more conscious and formalized transmission. The diagram below reiterates what has just been said about the process that seems to give rise to "culture" in the commonest sense of the term:

Figure 1: Culture basic constituents

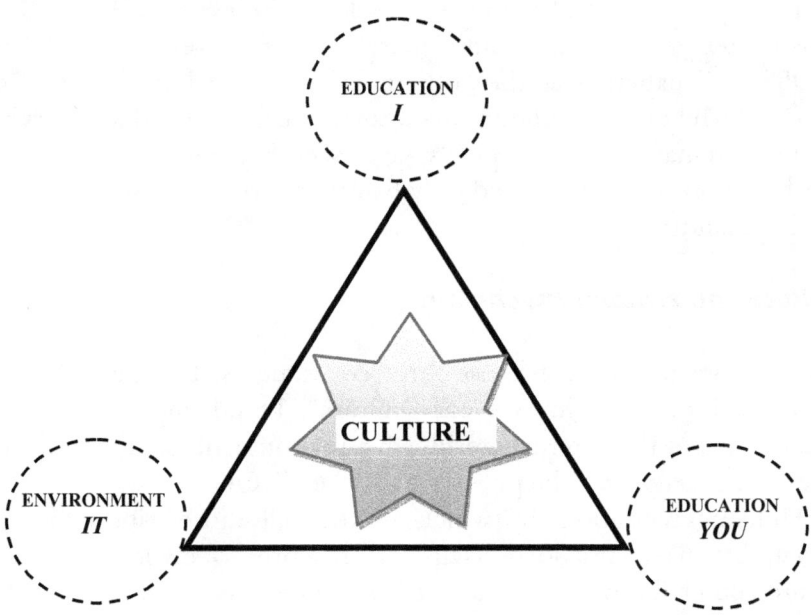

The first pole represents the first constituent of culture, namely the ENVIRONMENT. This is the first matrix that hosts the living organism in which its learning and development will take place. The environment is thus this thing which stimulates it by hindering it and provides the first elements from which it draws its energy. The phase is coined as "IT". When biological evolution leads the living entity to experience its separation from the environment-matrix, with this animate object/living entity designated as "IT", the living entity becomes capable of learning and transmission and optimization of its learning and transmission, it becomes "I". Then it develops the psychic structures which will lead to the emergence of self-consciousness, at the end of a learning process that goes from mechanical-unconscious to conscious-proactive. This is the "EDUCATION" pole of the graph. In this phase of development, "I" encounters another "I", something which is at the same time "IT" in its external manifestation, separated from the self and "I", in its resemblance and unity with self-consciousness. This is labelled "YOU". The "YOU" is the support of the transmission of the experience acquired by "I", but it is also the place where the future transformation of the experience of "I" takes place. "YOU" is the receptacle of the experience but also the transformer of the latter and therefore, of its evolution. Through "YOU", "I" experiences the "otherness" which is both self and other than self. The other condition of success, satisfaction and self-survival as Maslow remarks: "The needs of security, property, love and considerations can be satisfied only by others'. It is the "EXPERIENCE " pole of culture.

Culture and Human Psychology

The relationship between these three constituents, IT, I, and YOU, are the foundations of what we call "culture". Freud, in his definition of culture, evokes the external world, "the environment" and the relation to others, in other words the poles of "IT" and "YOU":

Human civilization, by which I mean all those aspects in which human life has embedded itself and I scorn to distinguish between culture and civilization... It includes all the necessary steps which should be taken in order to adjust the relations between the two parties, of men to one another and especially the distribution of available wealth. (Freud, 1927, pp. 5-6- *Future of illusion*).

In *Civilization and its discontents*, he adds a third element, the "body", as a source of suffering against which Man seeks to protect himself. The body can be identified to a certain extent to "I" since it is its first representation.

These three external elements, IT, I and YOU, constitute the minimal atomic structure of the living being and consequently the bases of the structuring of the human psyche. They can be related to the three psychic instances of Freud, "IT" being largely responsible for the constitution of Id, "I" being able to be assimilated to the Freudian Ego. If these two instances are primary instances, Freud stipulates that the superego is formed in contact with the parents and all that, at one time or another and reflect the model. What this shows us is simply that the superego is formed in contact with another ego, an alter-ego. That's what we have called "YOU". According to Freud, this "YOU" is more of a parent or a figure that reflects the model (educators, teachers, idols, etc.). We consider that what matters here is the experience acquired through age, knowledge, status and which is synonymous with the presence of a specific knowledge for the ego to enable it to attain a certain ideal.

As Freud defines it, Id/IT would be the earliest instance which would emerge from the "original chaos," the primordial energy that develops and complexifies according to the law of natural evolution and gives birth to the first phase of consciousness, the "I/ Ego". The arrival on the stage of another "I / Ego", an alter-ego (YOU), will sometimes help to occasionally counteract the impulses and desires of I / Ego, for the best interests of the group (I and You). In these circumstances, it is not surprising that the Superego/Experience is the basis of the constitution of "Culture", since it is also "What really binds men together - the ideas and the standards they have in common" Ruth Benedict (1959: 14); or as Ward Goodenough (1971: 19) states, it refers to "what is learnt, ... the things one needs to know in order to meet the standards of others."

If we have used basic Freudian psychology in this study, it is only to facilitate the interpretation of concepts used here and by no means an acceptance of the Freudian global conception of culture. Carl Jung's reading of the human psyche and human evolution as a process of elevating self-consciousness, seems to us more in keeping with the theory of culture set out in this article.

Figure 2: Consciousness stratums and co-evolution

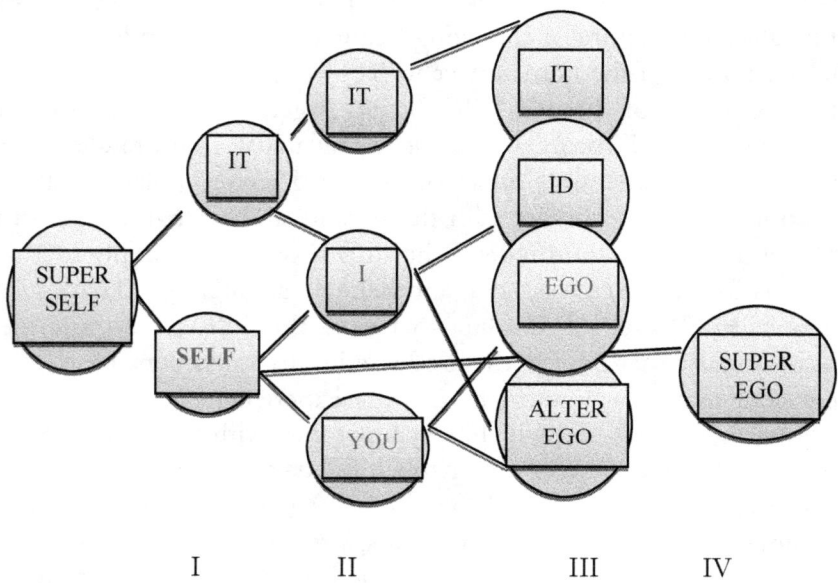

I   II   III   IV

This figure 2 summarizes what has been said above and should be read as follows. The Super-Self, which manifests itself in archetypal form in all creation, is the energy that exists in everything, even in matter. It becomes denser and in its extreme point gives the raw material, IT, but in this form the archetype of the Super-Self becomes the Self, separating from IT, even though it is identical to it in essence as ice and vapor are of the same essence or as the sound-image signifier is different from the tangible signified. But the two elements are absorbed in the concept or idea of the sign (Super-Self). Densification, which is the inverse process of individuation in Jung, produces interacting body layers whose core remains a pure archetypal form of the Super-Self. Just as the concept of "tea" materializes phonetically first in [ti] and then in the form of a particular drink.

In this diagram, we observe four successive levels of evolutions from a Jungian perspective, the first level being that of the Super-Self, corresponding to the Jungian Self, the source of creation and the primordial noûs. The access, through the process of individuation, according to Jung, causes the "numinous" phenomenon.

The second level is the first densification corresponding to the first manifestation or exteriorization of the Super-Self in the "intelligible" world, in a Platonic sense. The Self remains pure representation of the Super-Self, the core of the new form, surrounded by a first body (IT), which will experience a double thickening (in one part ending up in the individual raw materials and on a second part leading up to refinement of living forms which could be observed to be increasingly evolved). With each thickening, the body is modeled by the Self, to allow it the ability to obtain the most comprehensive measure of expressions. This process of body modeling to achieve this goal is the one that is the basis of natural selection.

At the microscopic level, the third stage is associated with the appearance of the first living organism. Even if the awareness of "the other" as such is not great for micro-organisms, the idea of "cooperation" or "competition" is already present in the cells. At the level of the human being, this level remains unconscious, in the form of an "individuality" felt but not assumed, the seat of desires and memories repressed or forgotten, memory of the whole process of "densification-individuation" self. The social and assumed part of the "I" is presented in the form of the EGO, the personality. While Id represents these drives and desires which formed and treated during the last phase of the individual's life, since his childhood. These desires and drives combine and interact with older ones and are part of the long process of evolution of the individual.

The last phase refers particularly to the human being. If the social animals experiment a part of it, it simply shows that the Super-Self is already present in the genetic program of the living being. If the bees could communicate the reason could be understood to be the fact that they have a task sharing code and they are forced to do so. The Super-ego cannot grow enough to become aware of its source and get its full expression through institutionalized culture.

In Human Beings, on the other hand, the Super-Ego is born in the interstice of the Ego and the Alter-ego. It is connected with the whole history of the evolution of the being, from the Self state until the appearance of the Ego and could be extended up to consciousness with the appearance of the Alter-ego. We can thus understand that the culture starts with at least two people. It is why certain religions state that the human history was initiated at the Earth with two humans slightly different: I (Ego) and You (Alter-ego). This religious story begins with innocence (unconsciousness) in individuality until the appearance of guilt with the desire aroused by duality (I and You). This guilt is actually a leap in evolution since it manifests the awareness of a pre-existing program, from which we must not deviate at the risk of stopping our evolution ... the stopping of evolution being the cause of the ultimate suffering (hell). Culture seems thus the means and ways to stick on to this program for evolution.

The Super-Ego is not to be confused here with the Freudian superego, the latter being a vague emanation of the first. Indeed, it exceeds the limits of early childhood in its formation. It is the register of the whole evolution of the living being, its impressions of the successes and failures during the long process of the appearance and development of life. It has in memory the problems, the difficulties, the pleasures and the sufferings of the living being since its appearance. Its substratum or more precisely its core being the Self, it is formed at the intersection of the Ego and the Alter Ego that share the Self, despite the inevitable differences in evolution. This is the common point between the two Egos and this is where culture is formed.

To sum up, at the intersection of I and YOU lies with the Self, the old and unconscious stratum of the living being, before the appearance of the Ego, who, after encountering an Alter-ego, prefigures the formation of the Super-Ego and the adventure to regain the Self from which it emerges. Culture is this adventure, this tension between the Ego and the Alter Ego to find the common place, namely the Self. Did Benda postulate anything else, as Finkielkraut[36] reports, when he regarded culture as "where the spiritual and creative activity of man takes place[37]"? Leading to the formation of a Super Self, which will be the steering mechanism for reaching the center for this objective.

3. Culture Variation

Change and cultural variations have been explained according to different theories of Darwinism and evolutionism such as Sociobiology (see Wilson, 1975, Dawkins, 1976, 1989, Lumsden & Wilson, 1981, Campbell, 1960, 1974, 1976), Environmentalism such as the adaptationist approach (Hawkes, O'Connell, & Rogers, 1997, Borgerhoff Mulder, 2004) or the evolutionary psychology of John Tooby and Leda Cosmices 1992 or Hugo Mercier and Jean-Baptiste Van der Henst, 2007. These approaches have in common the fact of basing the cultural evolution on the natural selection of the most effective or the most adaptative behaviours. Most authors agree that "cultural traits", such as linguistic traits (phonetic and phonological) are spread through "mimicry", based on studies of learning among animals (such as birds' learning of song) and among mankind as far as human language is concerned. Our discussion here is not to comment on either the mimetic theory or the learning theory, but simply to share the idea that cultural change is the continuous process to achieve the best of choices.

If the factor that underlies cultural change can be the selection of the best choice, what explains the difference in human cultures? This theory, following the Darwinian theory of the evolution of species, comes to postulate the idea that cultures are different because they are not in the same phase of evolution. This error of view, born almost with Cultural Anthropology, has been called into question, as shown by this observation by one of the major contemporary anthropologists, Clifford Geertz (1973:345) [38]

> What, after all, is one to make of savages? Even now, after three centuries of debate on the matter-whether they are noble, bestialor even as you and I; if they do not, they are the only ones who have the right to be deceived. If their customs, from cannibalism to matriliny, are mere alternatives, no better and no worse, to our own, or crude precursors of our own now outmoded, or simply passing strange, impenetrable exotica amusing to collect; They are bound and we are free, we are bound and they are free-after all this we still do not know.

These Darwinian inspired theories do not explain cultural variations because there is no "tradition" that has not been influenced by another one. Besides, Malinowski had also introduced the idea that culture is based on the "needs" of the human being, in the sense of the psychologist Abraham Maslow. In the first stage of life, culture is a mean of subsistence, it is mechanical and the physical environment totally conditions it. It covers the physiological needs of feeding, reproduction, rest, living space. Only the law of genes is exercised in a compelling way and regulates the E3 (Environment-Education-Experience) system.

This phase could be called, by convenience, Primal Culture and corresponds to that of micro-organisms and plants whose social organization is minimal, even if its embryonic existence is increasingly observed and leaves no doubt today. The second phase is one in which a sound "socialization" is noticed, with behaviours such as the incidents when the other (another who at the same time different and similar) participates in the survival of the individual. This ranges from social hymenopteran (ants, bees, wasps) to large mammals. Cooperation between members of the species, rather than strict competition, plays a decisive role. It is the animalistic culture, whose main characteristics are cooperation and membership. It mainly covers security and belongingness related needs in Maslow's model.

While traditionally, Anthropology reserves culture only for human species, the development of ethological studies during the second half of the last century clearly showed that this distinction was not tenable. In addition to the aforementioned authors, Dominique Lestel, in his work entitled *Les origines animales de la culture*[39], demonstrates in great detail that there is no break between animals and humans in terms of cultural behaviour. Even traits that were thought to be purely human characteristics, such as bipedalism, empathy, sympathy, esteem, affectionate feelings can also be observed among animals, according to this author. Moreover, in most recent ethological studies, biologists and botanists begin to extend social behaviour to micro-organisms, such as bacteria and plants[40]. From these studies on animals, we can deduce that there is also learning, transmission and all the other behaviours which cover the physiological and psychological needs which have been mentioned above. Thus, it is difficult not to consider animals also as cultural beings, giving this term its most widely accepted meaning.

However, there is a need which seems peculiar to the human being, it is the last need in Maslow's "pyramid": the need for fulfilment, also called the need for self-realization or self-actualization by the psychologist. Maslow (1968: 65)[41]. explains this self-actualization as:

> ...a continual process of realizing their potentials, abilities and talents, which seems like the fulfilment of a mission (whether called destiny or vocation), increased knowledge and acceptance of the intrinsic nature of a person, as an incessant tendency towards unity, integration or synergy within an individual.

Maslow considers, on the whole, that the aim of this need is to enable "to be that what" the specific being "must be", to be faithful "to its own nature". He is one of the very few psychologists who have perceived this need of the human being. Mahrer (1968), another humanist psychologist, describes in his "five stages of development" the supreme necessity for Man to attain complete self-realization through a process of maturation and internalization of the "I" (Mahrer, id.)[42]. Thus, the need to actualize oneself is undoubtedly what specifies human culture in relation to animal culture and primal culture.

The first phase was centred on the "IT", in the sense that the living being is entirely dependent on its physical environment. The being (or the entity) is, in a way, alone in the face of nature and can only rely on his genetic material to survive. "Cultural" change takes place in a continuous process of selecting the best choice, which corresponds to the best adaptation to its environment.

The second phase is centered on the "YOU", where the living being finds an associate to be able to continue to live, this partner, who, was only a competitor in the first phase, becomes a useful partner with which one can negotiate in a strategy of " win-win ", whereas in the first phase the game played there is often a zero-sum one.

The third phase is centered on the "I", where a need which reinforces self-consciousness generally appears in the form of need to know oneself. This phase probably comes after the painful experience that even the partner asserts himself in certain circumstances as a competitor. The highest level in this last level will be to free oneself completely from "IT" and "YOU", so that its survival and satisfaction do depend entirely on the "I" alone so this could become the degree of achievement or more precisely, self-actualization. When basic life-sustaining needs are largely covered, when strong institutions guarantee the safety and rights of all, when the available education and knowledge enable the individual to manage his / her social life in a way that meets his or her needs of esteem and recognition, when art and leisure are sufficiently developed to enable the individual to rise above the terrestrial contingencies, when society allows the individual sufficient free time to learn, cultivate oneself to rise above formal institutions, then, we could have here some characteristics of phase three culture.

These phases are not segregated even if they follow each other in the evolution spectrum for the reason that is discussed above. But it is important to note that the human cultures which are observed on the planet favor one level or another according to their needs. All human cultures contain traits of each level, even if there are some needs which occupy the central place in each of the cultures. The culture emerging in a particularly restrictive context, may appear primitive or elementary, because it is mainly oriented towards the satisfaction of physiological needs. However, the members of this culture, because of their human nature, also feel the need for fulfillment and self-actualization, proper to the third level. The proof of this could be understood from the fact that it is only at this level that artistic creativity, harmony with nature and spiritual development are met.

But this specific observation regarding the reason which formulates the nature of the human members of any culture, attempting to explain the presence of the traits which are specific to the third level is not sufficient. Indeed, how can we explain that in a culture that seems to be deeply rooted in the basic needs of maintaining life (characteristics of levels 1 and 2), one can find an extremely refined and subtle art, as well as a cosmogony and a complex spiritual belief existing in the cultures which "seem" to be in the highest degree of culture? In fact, Jacques Soustelle[43] states there is no intelligible causal relationship between the rudimentary techniques of the Maya and their "prodigious intellectual refinement..."

This observation prompted us to revise the hierarchy which had been established by the old typological Anthropology, which conceived cultural evolution only according to a linear paradigm and to establish the superiority of one culture over the other. If biological evolution seems to have progressed in a linear way, from organic unconsciousness to greater consciousness, cultural evolution seems iterative, because of the impermanence of the environment that can transform a flourishing civilization into a heap of ruins (invasions, colonizations, natural disasters) and reversing the needs of survivors. Such a transformation re-emerges and brings to the forefront the cultural behaviors which are characteristic of the first level, while the cultural traits of the third which would have been developed later will come to the forefront, creating an unprecedented cultural situation with hybrid cultural behaviors. In such a situation, it is not uncommon to observe behaviors belonging to the primal or primary (survival and security) phase, coexisting with human-traits which have been described in "cognitive archeology" (cosmogonic and religious representations, modes of governance, medicinal knowledge and high artistic practices) that the profane observer will have difficulty in understanding the relationship and consistency.

Thus, when one observes a culture, he notices heterogeneous elements that come from different sources (environments and periods) but harmonized and unified, to meet the underlying principles of natural selection: the perpetuation of life, through the perfect adaptation to the existing environment through learning (education) and transmission (experience). This process of adaptation and learning, pushed to its ultimate stage, must lead the human individual to transcend the constraints of the physical universe in order to regain his state of primitive individuation in full consciousness. This is essentially the goal of individuation in Jung ['s] conception, as he points out here:

> The path of individuation means: tending to become a truly individual being and, in so far, as we mean by individuality, the form of our most intimate uniqueness, our last and irrevocable uniqueness, it is the

realization of the characteristics of Oneself, in what it has the most personal and most rebellious aspects to any comparison.[44]

The great human civilizations, of which we have sufficient testimony, have brought to this level their cultural exigencies. It is also the highest meaning of the term "culture" in connection with the "education of the mind". But, it is difficult to say whether among these known civilizations, one has ever reached the ultimate stage of "individuation", in the Jungian sense of the term, by making it a general orientation of all of its members. The most common case we encounter is the existence of a priestly class "oriented mainly towards this ultimate goal of individuation ". The social function of this class is to enable the rulers and the people to benefit from their experiences and knowledge, often making it appear that the process of individuation cannot be possible to be inclusive of the general masses but is the privilege of a certain social class or even of some privileged and chosen ones.

4. Towards a Culture of Spirit

Based on the analysis above, we have defined three major phases of cultural evolution: the primal stage, the animal stage and the human stage, which are defined by the types of major needs in each stage. These needs correspond to a certain state of the morphogenetic evolution of the living being. Merlin Donald, a professor of cognitive psychology, proposed a scenario based on four cultural stages: the episodic stage with the primates (chimpanzees, bonobos and orangutans), the mimic stage of Homo erectus, the mythical stage of Homo sapiens, Archaic and Homo Neanderthalensis and finally, the stage of the theoretical culture of Homo sapiens. In this scenario, there is of course the assumption that culture begins with primates, which goes against the thesis explained here.

But by following the same type of reasoning as Merlin, one can identify the driving factors of each of the stages of the evolution such as the primal stage, where culture is mechanical-mimetic and is all centered on IT, YOU is not yet. Evolution is totally unconscious. For many we are at the zero level of culture, although the device underlying the emergence of culture is already there, what Teilhard de Chardin called "the Matter Spirit".

In the animal stage, where the culture is mimetic, the YOU begins to be perceived. When in this same stage, the culture is refined and becomes symbolic, it is a culture centered on the YOU. In the last stage, the culture becomes aesthetic and focuses on the "I".

In the mechanical culture, the main motivation of culture is adaptation to the environment, in the mimetic culture, the stake is the expansion towards the other; in the symbolic culture, the desires of Human beings become their emancipation from the other, after gradually emancipating itself from the environment and in the aesthetic culture, it is a matter of realizing oneself or actualizing one's Self. The last two phases are exclusively related to the human beings.

This description of culture in three (or four) phases can only show the uninterrupted continuity of creation, from the mineral and preorganic phase including the "pre-life", to the organic-animal phase and the human phase. It is too crude to reflect the evolution of culture within human societies. On the other hand, it indicates the dynamics involved in the most elementary forms of creation as well as the most evolved form of consciousness, described as the phase of the 'integrated man', the man realized, the cosmos-centered research observations of Don Edward Beck and Christopher Cowan (1996).

5. Conclusion

It is almost a reflex to define culture by its products or manifestations, which is a tautological way to answer the question: What is culture? What is music? It's an art? What is agriculture? It is also an art, like literature, painting, etc. And religion, customs, beliefs, games, production techniques are all products of culture. What is their common denominator? It is because it allows the human being to live, to improve his/her life, to increase the quality of it. In short, the common dominator is their finality.

As Malinowski, Linton, Kluckhohn and Redfield have advocated, there is an actual common core of cultural values in all societies, which derives from the universal functions of satisfying human needs and aspirations which could be understood to be the finality. There are concrete cultural, universal values because there are universal needs, biological, derived and integrative, common to all societies. These cultural universes are not merely abstract categories but actual regulative modes of conduct and norms of conduct which are common to all cultures. Such transcultural values may be called absolutes as well as universals. Cultural relativists tend to stress cultural differences but neglect the uniformities and common elements.

Ken Wilber, in his theory of Integral Culture, develops the idea that individual men as well as the human society in general passes through four phases, egocentric (selfish, which recalls the selfishness of pre-organic phase), ethnocentric, worldcentric and at last integrated. He shares this evolutionary conception of consciousness with Don Edward Beck and Christopher Cowan (1996) who formalized the thought of their master C. Graves (1950) in the form of an ascending spiral which passes through eight phases of evolution.

This conception of the evolution of human beings and societies, which is just a continuation of cosmological and biological evolution, has been envisaged since the 1930s-40s and especially in the 1950s. Many scientists have been trying to establish a global theory of evolution of life (Dobzhansky, Theodosius, 1937; Julian Huxley, 1942; Teilhard de Chardin, 1955; George Gaylord Simpson, 1949; Julian Huxley and Ernst Mayr, 1955, etc.) From all these works, we can deduce that culture is a dynamic that allows man to perfect all his faculties: physical, mental and spiritual.

Finally, to specify cultures of different nations, we can see them through an analogy: cultures of human beings are like fruit trees of different kinds, growing up in different geographical conditions. Certain trees seem flourishing, bearing fruits and flowers, some others are green with plenty of flowers but have no visible fruits on their branches, some are small, struggling with the elements, because they have been cut so many times to be used as comestible. Indeed, under these little trunks, we can discover shells of fruit but only trained eyes can discern them. To find again fruits on these tree trunks, we must let them develop themselves, where development could take centuries, even millennia.

But time will not let any indigenous culture develop itself in the new global and open environment nowadays. A monolithic culture is emerging and imposing itself on all other cultures, through the new technologies of communication. All cultures are genetically modified as a sudden. Those who understand the dynamic of culture in general and this global culture in particular will take advantage of it to achieve their goal.

The principal opponent of this cultural dynamism is indeed religion which is caught in its own contradiction: to achieve the highest degree of culture, namely "perfection of man", but at the same time refusing to him the possibility to change whereas his environment is constantly changing. The principal support of this cultural dynamic, on the other hand, is science, but only the science which which could go beyond the materialistic paradigm on which it has been based on since the sixteenth century.

References

[1] Radcliffe-Brown Alfred R., (1952) *Structure and Function in Primitive Society: Essays and Addresses.* London: Cohen & West; Glencoe, III.: Free Press.

[2] Redfield Robert (1962 and 1963:papers7: 2, p. 107), Edited by Margaret Park Redfield, The University of Chicago Press.

[3] Tylor, E. in Seymour-Smith, C. (1986), *Dictionary of Anthropology.* The Macmillan Press LTD.

[4] http://www.unesco.org/most/migration/glossary_cultural_diversity.htm / 31 Oct. 2015

[5] Lawrence A. Lowell (1915), "The North American Review", Vol. 202, No. 719 (Oct., 1915), pp. 553-559, published by University of Northern Iowa Stable URL: http://www.jstor.org/stable/25108618, p. 553.

[6] Kroeber Alfred L. and Kluckhohn Clyde (1952), *Culture: A Critical Review of Concepts and Definitions*. Harvard University Peabody Museum of American Archeology and Ethnology Papers, Vol. 47, No. 1. Cambridge, Mass.: The Museum. A paperback edition was published in 1963 by Vintage Books. The emphasis is from the author of this article.

[7] White Leslie A. (1959), *The Concept of Culture*. American Anthropologist, 61(2), 227–251.

[8] Cf.Finkielkraut Alain, *la défaite de la pensée* (1987), Paris, Gallimard.

[9] Boas Franz (1940), *Race, Language and Culture* New York, Maxmillan.

[10] Sapir Edward (1985), *Selected Writings in Language, Culture, and Personality*, University of California Press.

[11] Lévi-Strauss Claude, (1952), *Race et histoire*, Ed. Unesco.

[12] Cf. Vassiliki Betty Smocovitis, *Current Anthropology* (2012), "*Humanizing Evolution: Anthropology, the Evolutionary Synthesis and the Prehistory of Biological Anthropology, 1927–1962*", Vol. 53, No. S5

[13] Dion-Stout Madeleine and Kipling Gregory (2003), *Aboriginal People, Resilience and the Residential School Legacy*, Ed.Aboriginal Healing Foundation, Canada.

[14] In German, the term *Kultur* means culture and civilisation at the same time.

[15] Freud Sigmund (1930), *Civilization and its discontents*. SE, 21: 64-145. The emphasis on certain words is from the author of this article.

[16] Malinowski Bronislaw (1944), *A Scientific Theory of Culture and Other Essays*, Chapel Hill, The University of North Carolina Press, p. 120.

[17] *Op. cit.*, p. 36. We underline this sentence ourselves.

[18] Beck Lewis White (1986), *Kant On history*, Macmillan/Library of Liberal Arts.

[19] Lévi-Strauss, Claude (1981), *Culture et nature*, « La condition humaine à la lumière de l'anthropologie», in Commentaire, no 15, automne, p. 367.

[20] The term is related with the Greek word "mimeme" which means *imitation*. The memes which are cultural traits reduplicates as genes but on the basis of imitation.

[21] Dawkins Richard, *id.*, p.62.
[22] This idea of macro-genes is relevant with that which sees « Culture » as super-organic (*cf. Kroeberg*).
[23] Matsumoto David (1996), *Culture and Psychology*. Pacific Grove, CA: Brooks/Cole.
[24] The words in bolt refers to *information*, the underlined term to the *transmission* and the "group of people" to a specific *environment*.
[25] Laland Kevin N. and Bennett G. Galef, Eds (2009), *The Question of Animal Culture*. Cambridge, Mass: Harvard UP.
[26] Matsuzawa Tetsurō, Masaki Tomonaga, and M. Tanaka (2006), *Cognitive Development in Chimpanzees*. Tokyo: Springer.
[27] Tyler John Bonner (1980), *The Evolution of Culture in Animals*. Princeton University Press, Princeton
[28] Rendell Luke and Whitehead Hal (2001), "Culture in Whales and Dolphins", *The Bavioral and Brain Sciences*, 24. 2 (2001): 309-24.
[29] In Hilaire Giron, 2015, Teilhard, visionnaire d'un monde en évolution : du Big -Bang à la Noosphère, conférence n°4265, Bull. n°45, pp. 67-84 2014- *Bulletin de l'Academie des sciences et lettres de Montpellier*
[30] Weismann August (1893), *The germ-plasm; a theory of heredity*.New York: Scribner's.
[31] Winnicott Donald W. (1953), Transitional Objects and Transitional Phenomena—A Study of the First Not-Me Possession, International Journal of Psycho-Analysis, 34:89-97.
[32] Bertalanffy Ludwig. v. (1969/1976). General Systems Theory: Foundations, Development, Applications (Revised Edition). New York: George Braziller, Inc. (p. 39-40).
[33] Gidley Jennifer M. (2013), L'évolution de la conscience et le changement de paradigme », IN La nouvelle Avant-garde, vers un changement de culture, Sous la direction de CarineDartiguepeyrou, L'Harmattan Collection Avant-garde, 2013.
[34] Some revolutionary biologists consider that there are smaller living organism such as microzymas (Antoine Béchamp, or protits (Günter Enderlein), or somatides (Gaston Naessens)

[35] Atkinson Richard C. & Shiffrin Richard M., (1968), Human memory." A proposed system and its control processes", In K. Spence & J. Spence (Eds.), *The psychology of learning and motivation*. Princeton, NJ: Van Nostrand.

[36] Finkielkraut Alain (1989), *Ladéfaite de la pensée, id.* :.13.

[37] «…là où se déroulel'activitéspirituelleetcréatrice de l'homme ».

[38] Geertz Clifford (1973), *The Interpretation of Cultures, Selected Essays*, Ed. Basic Books, Inc., Puhlishers, New York.

[39] Lestel Dominique (2001), *Les origines animales de la culture,* Ed. Flammarion, Paris.

[40] Cf. Cordero Otto (2009), Stuart West (2007), etc.), and cf. Dudley (2009), for plants.

[41] Maslow Abraham (1968), *Toward A Psychology of Being*, Van Nostrand, New York.

[42] Mahrer, Alvin. R. (1989), *Experiencing: A humanistic theory of psychology and psychiatry.* Ottawa, Canada: University of Ottawa Press, p.785-834.

[43] Soustelle Jacques (1967), *Les quatre soleils*, Paris, Pion, (Collection « Terre Humaine »), p.107.

[44] Jung Carl (2001), *Dialectique du Moi et de l'inconscient*, Folio Essais, p. 115 *«La voie de l'individuation signifie : tendre à devenir un êtreréellementindividuel et, dans la mesureoù nous entendons par individualité la forme de notreunicité la plus intime, notreunicitédernière et irrévocable, ils'agit de la réalisation de son Soi, danscequ'il a de plus personnel et de plus rebelle à toutecomparaison. »*

CHAPTER TWO

Cultural Dimension in State Building: Focus on Somali Case

Part 1- The Past as a Mirror

1. Introduction

Preamble

In a review of an article written by Ahmed I. Samatar (2001)[45], Ali Jimale[46] recalls the metaphor of the man who has lost the key to his house and was looking for it under a street-lamp, but without finding it. When he was asked if he was sure he lost it there, he replied "No!", and pointed his finger towards a remote dark place. So, why was he looking for it at that place? "Because', he said, "there is no light over there." From that, Jimale concludes his comments:

> Perhaps that is what we all are doing: looking for answers in a place much traveled. After all, human footprints give solace to the traveler. And herein, lays the irony: the path trailblazed by early footprints deny the new traveler the courage to survey a new path. Talk about dictatorships! We are still beholden to the past, whether it is anthropology, I.M. Lewis, clannism or Somali tradition. The time has perhaps come to initiate a new way of looking at things, a new way that could take us away from the place lit by a solitary circle of light.

I do not know what Jimale had in mind when he was saying "to initiate a new way of looking at things", but it is, in fact, what is fundamentally needed today to really "restore hope" amongst Somalis. I am aware of the tremendous challenge this proposition represents, but at the same time, the approach proposed here is in no way revolutionary, since it has an explicit and well-known theoretical basis. It corresponds to a pragmatic approach which is deep-rooted in the modus vivendi culture which is dear to the Somalis.

Dominant Narrative

There is a dominant narrative in the presentation of Somali history from the 60s until today, which is somewhat consistent with the principles of classical historiography. We are told how certain events gave rise to some other events, which, in a continuous series of causes and effects, gave birth to the present situation of the Somalis. For instance, many scholars and analysts explain that Somalia's central government collapsed because of the discrepancy between the Somali clan mode of organization and the newly adopted democratic system which had first led to a chaotic governance and then to the political coup of 1969 and the dictatorship of Siyad Barre. The latter, due to the clan manipulation system of governance put in place by the regime itself, led progressively to the final failure of the Central government on 1991. And it is after lessons learnt from that experience, that, a federal system of governance was adopted after the year 2000. This is a kind of official story which can be read here and there and that most people have in mind, even if some scholars have tried their best to mitigate this narrative (cf. Ahmed I. Samatar, 2001). The postulate behind this interpretation of events is that man makes history. Our assumption, however, is that nature makes history and man tells stories about it and we will try to show how, through the concept of "the Somali Unity Political Project" (labelled SUPP here) and its evolution.

The idea will be, first, to illustrate how all along the decades and centuries, history seems to portray this unity in a certain way and how Somalis, during all the last century, have tried to portray it in another way. This gap, creating continuous discordance and disharmony, led up to the final collapse of the Republic of Somalia.

We will then move the discussion forward from the perspectives of how to move forward with the historical dynamism manifested amongst Somalis and also in the world and how to maintain or reinforce this informal but yet powerful unity of the Somali nation. To do this, we will introduce a new paradigm about Somaliness, based on one of the most extraordinary components of Somali heritage: the *xeer-dhaqameed* (traditional law). This law emphasizes that hard work starts from the ground: *hanta guntaa laga toolaa* ("a wooden bucket is sewn from the bottom").

Theoretical Background

1- We can look at an impressionist painting very closely to consider its composition, by paying particular attention to the way the artist links forms, plays with colors, draws outlines, uses various materials, etc. and we will draw from it a particular meaning and purpose. On the other side, if we take a step back to try to perceive the whole scene, to embrace the totality of the work, we will have another narrative. History appears like this impressionist painting, in that historians and analysts try to account for the details of the facts, to establish their links and streamline the relations. But we also need to step back to apprehend the whole historical trend, to grasp the importance and position of each element and the real meaning of the full scene.

2- This approach can be justified by the parable of the elephant and the blind persons; each grabs a part of the elephant and tries to describe the whole from the part he/she has touched. The moral of this story being, that it is the view of the whole that makes it possible to understand each of the parts and not the opposite. This is why we have chosen to consider the history of the Somali nation from an evolutionary approach that will serve us both as a promontory and as a tool for interpretations. The sequential analysis of historical facts cannot be denied, but the understanding of these facts can only emerge in reality through a holistic or systemic capture, which is able to better account for the complexity of the considered phenomena and their interactions. Just as the meaning of a sentence is not reduced to the sum of the meanings of the elements it contains in a similar manner, history of a period cannot be reduced to a set of facts observed during this same period.

In his sociological treatise written in 1985, Omar. O. Rabeh[47] considers that "the most original theory and the deepest ... is the one that assimilates society to a living organism and integrates it into animal kingdom". This view is on the same line as Espinas (1844-1922) who postulates that "it is necessary (...) to admit that Sociology is simply the continuation and the blooming of Biology, that human society is a concrete and living thing in the same way as the animal societies".[48] Indeed, Man, let alone societies, is not outside the global movement of life. Even if the movements of galaxies, planets, societies and humans are not found in the same time scale, they all participate to this evolution of life that Teilhard de Chardin describes in the *Human Phenomenon*.[49] In the same vein, we have defended the idea that human culture is situated at a particular phase of the general evolution of terrestrial life, oriented towards a greater consciousness.

This postulate takes us further away from the classical historiography which is akin to a deciphering of an unknown language and brings us closer to a historiography integrated into the global evolutionary process, which would be similar to a semantic analysis of a text of a known language. The difference is tiny but decisive. In the first, it is a matter of finding out or constructing the first meaning of the text, in the other one, of understanding the real aim of the author in the text, the real meaning which, lies beyond the materiality of the text as its literal meaning. The two approaches intersect in certain areas, but differ in their means and methods. We are aware of the immensity of the work to be done, the numerous risks of falling into elementary determinism if a rigorous epistemology does not mark the method and the path. But there is one clear epistemological fact that historiography cannot continue to ignore: history precedes Man, just as culture did not begin with Man. And for that reason, the compartmentalization of the world objects, the separations established in the continuum of life and time, justified or not by the methodological simplicity of an epistemology based on a fragmented world, does not hold up any longer. So, let us take the liberty of telling the story from its other direction, the one described by evolutionists such as Teilhard de Chardin, Ken Wilber and others (*see* Part I.). The sum of knowledge accumulated during the human historical period, in various fields of research, is considerable enough to conceive, with Teilhard de Chardin, that the arrow of time is directed towards the Spirit. If so, why not look at history from this perspective?

3- Moreover, the causal relations that we establish between events are not always objective; in any case, they are not the only "valid" ones such as Paul Watzlawick[50], Ernest Von Glarsesfeld[51] and other constructionists following these pioneers, have shown. This is the reason why the history of Sayid Mohamed Abdallah Hassan gave rise to several radically opposed interpretations according to the authors' outlook (Abdisalam M. Issa-Salwe[52], John P. Slight[53], Cabdiraxmaan C. Faarax , "Barwaqo"[54], Yasiin C. Kenedid[55], Aw Jaamac C. Isse[56]). This is not to justify anarchistic relativism of historical facts, but the possibility of looking at history itself differently. If Hegel has claimed, in his *Philosophy of History*, that Africa has no history[57], it is because he had a particular perception of history. History, in the sense of successions of events, describing the past of a person or a nation, which could have been chronologically and carefully recorded in books, does not, in fact, makes much sense in traditional African societies. This history, still conveyed in textbooks illustrating the biographical narrative of ego-nations or ego-individuals, is a recently borrowed perception in Africa. The egotistical formation of a nation or an individual, with his desires, his fears, his frustrations, his conquests, his defeats, have no meaning in themselves, if they do not leave a lesson in life, a morality, a teaching beyond the facts reported. In this context, Africans may not have a history, but they have stories. Such stories could give rise to maxims, proverbs, sayings such as those of the Somali 'mythical' figures, Bucur Bacayr, Wiil Waal or Caraweelo, for which we have no factual evidence of their existence. However, their stories are still sources of inspiration and recreation for Somalis who use the sayings or proverbs attributed to them in various circumstances of their daily lives.

4- Moreover, it seems that the classic historiographical approach, which has the advantage of simplicity, shows itself as extremely reductive when not all the facts contributing to an event are recorded. There are circumstances which could be considered as being worthy to be relegated to that of the measure of "secondary importance" and are not recorded or not recordable (because they are too complex or seem fortuitous) but actually participate in the historical phenomena. Montesquieu speaks of "particular incidents"[58] which could contribute to the emergence of a particular cause. "Particular incidents" may appear to be incidental to the analysists, but without them, the course of history would be different. It is the "Cleopatra's nose effect" in Roman history, precursor of the "butterfly effect" developed in physics theory.

5- The Republic of Somalia has shifted from being a core nation in the greater Horn of Africa to…not even a peripheral nation, but to a failed country which is now struggling to become a peripheral nation. But there is a race against the clock engaged between the other core countries of the Horn which wanted to attract and extend their influence[59] to the peripheral elements of the failed core. From this perspective, the northern Somalia (Somaliland) and the South West of Somalia are in the process of being swallowed in the ever expanding influence of Ethiopia, according to the implications of the Core-periphery theory[60], whereas Kenya's influence in the extreme south of Somalia (Jubaland) is strengthening, according to the same theory.

6- We need to go back to the dark place where we have lost the key. The dark place is that which classical historiography has difficulty to account for, since its methodology seems inadequate to capture relations which are impalpable, moving and fluidic. Seeing in this dark place requires a more intuitive sense of perception than an analytical approach, since our super-rationalized minds, trained to separate things, are unable to grasp any meaning from the myriad of facts it has identified.

7- At last, this approach does not recognize chance as an operational tool to report history understanding history, neither are coincidences. Rather, paraphrasing Durkheim[61], chance and coincidences are only abstract products of "the reasoning mind which finds its limits." When Socrates says "all that I know is that I know nothing" this is indeed more about the method of knowing which he would like to share than a statement of lack of knowledge. If we notice that in 2017, exactly one century after the inauguration of the French sponsored railway Djibouti-Addis, the new railway sponsored by China was inaugurated in Djibouti, while the old one has been abandoned, is this a mere chance ? What does that mean? We will answer like Socrates, we do not know, but let us see....

2. Somalia Central State Collapse: The Diagnosis

The Wide Spread Interpretation

There is a wide spread and dominant interpretation of Somali modern history and, especially, about the collapse of Somalia's central government in 1991. We can find this interpretation expressed in Catherine Wanjiku Nyambura's article (2011)[62], where she quotes Somali and non-Somali authors who share her views. She says:

> The democratic principles were being enacted at the top level while nepotism, corruption and clan competition were rapidly eroding the underpinnings of Somalia's nascent democratic system. The Political misrule, combined with pervasive corruption, hampered the maturity of administrative institutions and undermined development of the country's embryonic social services network, thereby engendering general disillusionment with the entire system (Abdulle & Ali, 2004). The exploitation of clan identity by political opportunists swiftly gave rise to an unwieldy number of clan based political parties...

This kind of statement is frequent in the literature about Somalia's collapse[63]. Indeed, this analysis, as the others along the same lines[64], seems to be based on field work observations, well-documented facts and rational analysis. Indeed, the diagnosis seems logical and the arguments are so obvious that everyone automatically accepts the solutions preconized and expressed by the author as such:

> For peace to prevail, the research found out that Somalia should first involve all the conflicting parties, both internal and external, in their peace negotiations. To further improve security, the outlawed groups and civilians should be disarmed and Somalis should be encouraged to join together for peace and speak in one voice to end the conflict. The international community should as well be cautious of financing individual clans, militia and other interest groups involved directly in conflict. They should be engaged in dialogue with the warring parties without taking sides and support an outcome that would lead to the achievement of sustainable peace...[65]

The only thing is that this diagnosis mistakes smoke for fire and the solution is thus necessarily foggy. Second, this scenario of Somalia State failure is built on the curious assumption that all Somali political leaders from the independence until today have failed[66] "due to irresponsible policy, power greed and corruption"[67] or because under their governance" power and access to it was pursued as an opportunity to promote, at the state and sub-state levels, the vested interests of the given class and/or clan to which that elite belonged ».[68] And of course, the worst of them was Siyad Barre who ransacked the country because it brought to a pinnacle all the defects of Somalia: clannism, social conservatism, nepotism, the will of territorial conquest, etc. We do not share this analysis.

In this article, we assume that all the flaws mentioned here are not the causes of the failure of the Somala as a state and its difficult recovery, but some of the logical effects of a project which has been going against the trend of history for almost one century. This project has run with more or less speed and when it reached its greatest acceleration from 1978, it simply totally collapsed less than fifteen years later. And indeed, the driver of the state car at that time was Siyad Barre, it is why he is fingered out more than the politicians before him, although he has only been acting according to the historical trend that brought him to power.

New Diagnosis: Yesterday is not behind [69]

The past is too strong with us and we cannot erase its bitter memories when its ill-effects stare us glaringly at every twist and turn - in the economic, social, political, cultural and religious spheres. Our people have been treated as cattle in the past. They were deprived of their lands forcibly and without compensation...Thousands were made homeless and whereas a few of them escaped, the majority of them - men and women and children - were all seized and forced to toil as slaves...." SYL 9 June 1949, the Central Committee of the SYL

What is this project, how and why has it run against the trend of history, as we have said previously? This project is the "Somali union Political project" (SUPP) which was dreamed about by Somalis for generations, which was the main priority of the initial Somali governments, which is still turning like a leitmotiv in the minds of millions of Somalis. It is the biggest issue for which the Federal State of Somalia (FSS) has to find a solution in order to go forward and open a new era for Somalis.

This means that after more than one century of struggle for unity, this has not been achieved. Worse, it even seems that what had been gained after 1960 has in the last decades been wasted. In fact, if we try to assess Somali national unity in present days, with objective criteria, we will notice striking similarities between the situations of the Somalis in the period from the second half of the 19th century up to the 1920s.

Indeed, there is a Somali state, internationally recognized, but this state is embryonal and is challenged by internal and external forces which tremendously weaken its actions. It is battling for its own survival and has no real power over its entire territory. That put aside, if we consider a) the political configuration of Somali territories, b) the powers in competition in these territories, c) the strongest and most visible opposition against foreign presence in Somali territories, d) the spirit of *soomaalinimo* or the idea of ethnic unity among Somalis, e) the control of Somali affairs, we can see a strange parallelism between the two periods as depicted in the maps and table below:

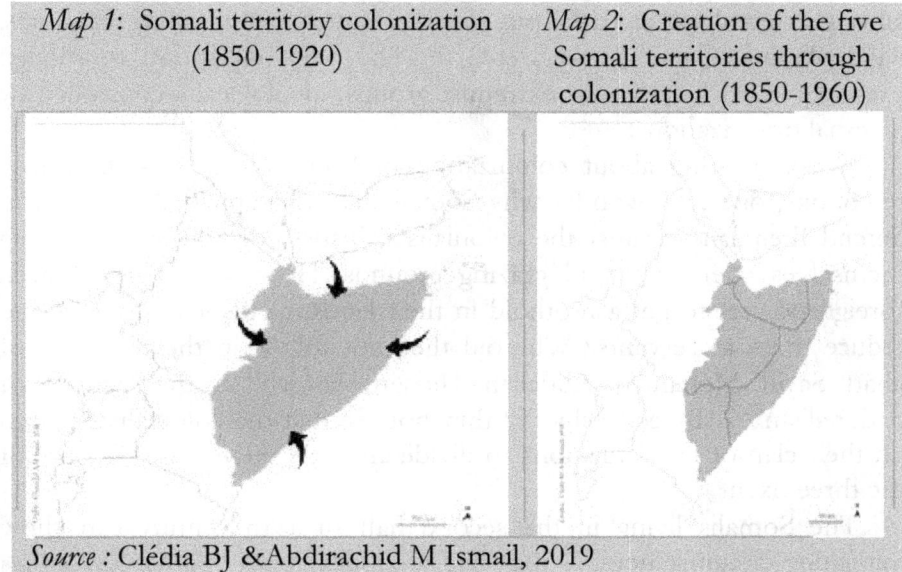

Map 1: Somali territory colonization (1850-1920)

Map 2: Creation of the five Somali territories through colonization (1850-1960)

Source : Clédia BJ &Abdirachid M Ismail, 2019

Table 1: Striking similarities between two periods

	1850-1920	1991-Today
Somalis territories	Five regions	Five different entities[70]
Powers in competition	Ethiopia, Turkey, Egypt, Western powers	Ethiopia, Kenya, Western powers, Turkey, China, Gulf countries
Organized opposition to foreigner presence	Religious movements	Religious movements
Perception about "Somalihood" (Soomaalinimo)	Very weak Clan filiation stronger than ethnic filiation	Very weak Clan or political territory filiation stronger than ethnic filiation
Control of Somali affairs	Controlled by external powers	Controlled by external powers (either economically, politically or militarily)[71]

From this table, we can deduce that a) Somali territories are still divided into the five original regions; b) Somali clans are still competing with each other, each one having a specific treaty or relation with different foreign states; c) They are either under the protection of the previous colonial powers (or its African replacement) or under a new foreign power, d) They constitute a field of strong competition and rivalry among external forces (Ethiopia, Kenya, Unites States, China, Emirates, Saudi Arabia, Qatar, Turkey, etc.); e) The only opposition to foreign presence is led by religious extremist groups, ideologically controlled by external organizations.

When reading about colonization of Somali territories in history textbooks, one may wonder why Somalis had not united themselves to defend their land against the colonialists, instead of competing among themselves over wells and grazing grounds. How come they allowed foreign powers to get a foothold in their lands, to dispossess them and reduce them to servants? Why did they not follow in the footsteps of jihad Sayid Mohamed Abdallah Hassan, known as the symbol of nationalism[72] ? Indeed, why did they not see that the colonialists played on their clan or tribal filiations to divide and rule them, like the story of the three oxen?

The Somalis living in the second half of 19th century can show mitigating circumstances, as they had little idea about "Somali union" as a political concept, they had not in their memory any previous colonization or events regarding union and disunion processes and they had not experienced a golden era of "Soomaalinimo", like in the period between 1950 and 1975. But today, that is not the case, most Somalis and especially those elites who govern Somali territories, are aware of all of that[73], yet the same questions seem to be there and one "has the impression that current generations reproduce the same ideology and the same attitudes."[74]

However, every historical context has its specific issues which cannot be ascertained thoroughly from a remote place and time. And even if events seem comparable to a certain extent and that helps to understand them better, they are not of exactly the same nature since they are all rooted in specific space and time. That is why the Al Shabab movement, even if it may, to a certain extent, remind of the *Daraawiish* movement, is not reducible to the latter.

For that precise reason and not to reproduce the same errors constantly, we need to have a more precise picture on why and how the Somali Union has failed.[75]

How the SUPP has failed

Our objective here is not to draw a picture of all the historical processes which have led to the failure of the Somali Union Political Project (SUPP), but to highlight a few factors which need to be taken into account to explain this process. The first factor is the opposition between "Somali unity" and "Somali Union", the ethnic reality opposed to the historical and political project. The second is the colonization factor which has taken advantage of Somali social structure and the customary law about land and the third has been the ambiguity of the concept of "soomaalinimo", which has worked first as a mobilizing factor against colonization but has lost this "etic" meaning and have today almost an exclusive "emic" signification.

Somali Unity versus Somali Union

In fact, Somali unity refers to the Somali ethnic reality which, as David D. Laitin and Said Samatar (1987:29)[76] pointed out, is about "the fervent sense of belonging to a distinct national community with a common heritage and a common destiny [which] is rooted in a widespread Somali belief that all Somalis descend from a common founding father, the mythical Samaale to whom the overwhelming majority of Somalis trace their genealogical origin." But more specifically, what is Somali unity for a camel herder of Wajeer, a farmer of Jigjiga or a fisherman of Merka ? This will lead to the extreme and most curious paradox that something which already exists has to be sought: unity.

For Somalis, unity was and still is a given fact, not something to construct or to seek and this may explains why the trans-tribal term "Somali" appears comparatively late in the historical records.[77] In any case, Somalis were already conscious of their unity based on "language, way of life, predominately pastoral, a shared poetic corpus, a common political culture, a profound Islamic heritage[78]" and of course, as stated above, on their belief that they descend from a common source. And seeking or battling for what was already there was not something easy to conceptualize. If we examine recent history, it is a fact that the term "Somali" was specially and tremendously used to mobilize Somali clans against a foreign enemy, as was the case with Sayid Mohamed Abdalla

Hassan or with the SYL or again with the military regime of Siyad Barre.

We can now easily perceive where was the trouble: Somalis knew about their unity, which was a de facto ethnic reality, but what about "union"?...That was something out of their scope. We can unite what is separate, but how can we unite things or beings which are already "drawn together by emotive bonds of kinship and genealogical ties" (Latin and Said Samatar, Id.:21)?

One may consider that this question is linked to the clan organization of the Somali people, but not only to that. In fact, the question is much more about the gap between the scope of the "Somali Union Political Project" (SUPP), which prepares for a radically different mode of organization and the simplistic way this project was formalized, almost with only one word: "soomaalinimo". The leitmotiv was "union", but how to achieve this "union" or what sort of union the Somalis wanted, seems to have been swept aside, mainly for the reason developed in section 2.2.3.

It is why the humblest camel herder, the female milk seller, the most prominent intellectual or political leader have exactly the same opinion about this "union". It means for all of them: having one president, one government, one parliament, one country, one capital, for all the Somalis. It is why Somali politicians have strived for one century to achieve this goal, through several governments and two different political regimes and have all failed with more or less damage.   Instead of wondering about was wrong about the way the issue was tackled, instead of putting into question the SUPP as it was conceived, politicians and many intellectuals continue accusing tradition and culture[79] which, in fact, seem to reject this SUPP as an alien transplant – which, in fact, it was.

Colonization Factor

The western colonialists, observing the traditional political organizations of the Somalis and the peoples of the Horn in general, have simply taken advantage of it. What saved Ethiopia of Menelik from colonization did not exist in the Somali territories: a centralized power. The colonization has smoothly and perfectly matched the opportunities offered by Somali culture (and Afar culture as well), in terms of customary law, social and political organization, and antagonisms or inter-clanic competitions, which are neither worse nor better than interstate competition over scarce resources. Within a few years, the Somali nation was divided into five territories. At the very end of 19th and beginning of the 20th century, the anti-colonial resistance movements emerged among Somalis. One of the most outstanding movements was that of Sayid Mohamed Abdalla Hassan who who commenced his jihad in 1899.[80]

During this period, apart from the attacks of the Abyssinian army that routinely plunder the Somali inhabitants of Ogaden and Haud[81], the Somalis do not face a real conflict with the settlers. For the most part, they find their benefit in this situation. All the Somali clans seem to apply the law of modus vivendi to European foreigners who do not seem to be interested in two commodities dear to them: wells and pastures. The treaties they signed with them did not include "recognition of foreign domination" or a "cessation of any part of their territory". Lewis (1988) even states that the preambles to certain treaties, like the one signed with the English at the time of the departure of the Egyptians of Berbera and Bulhar, clearly mentioned that the Elders of Somali tribes were "desirous of entering into an Agreement with the British Government for the maintenance of [their] independence, the preservation of order and for the other good and sufficient reasons."[82]

But at the same time they declared that they would not enter into contact with other foreign powers, that they would "never give up, sell, mortgage or otherwise give for occupation, save to the British Government, any portion of the territory presently inhabited by them or being under their control."[83] Somali clans signed with colonial powers other treaties in which each party promised "maintaining and strengthening the relations of peace and friendship existing between them."[84]

Indeed as the interests of the colonial powers were growing and changing, they come to betray these treaties, as Lilius (2001:255)[85] reports: "It seems that the Europeans offered to treat the local leaders as sovereigns and representatives of states only the time needed to acquire some hold over a desired territory without having to fight for it. The fighting came only later, when the betrayal became obvious."

Thus colonization created borders amongst the Somali nation, but it did not succeed either in exacerbating the interclanic competitions or in repressing the consciousness of the filial unity of that nation. Even if France played on this register[86] by transforming, in 1967, the name of the territory it occupied, the French Somali Coast, into French Territory of the Afars and Issas (TFAI), it did not succeed in this project, since Somalia served as the home base of Djiboutian separatists, until Djibouti got its independence.

Suzanne Lilius (2001:260), quoting (Fitzgibbon, 1982:92-93), reminds that in 1940, "at the time of the UN investigation of the future of the Somalis and the Bevin plan, the Issas expressed the desire to join all the other Somalis in a common Somali state." And if Djibouti did not join Somalia in 1977, it is not that the unity of the Somali nation had been affected, but simply the fact that the Union project, which was against the Somali historical trend since its conception, as we will illustrate, had reached its final stage (cf. Suzanne Lilius, ibid.) The crucial role played by Djibouti in the affairs of the Horn of Africa since the Somali state collapsed, shows the relationship that the leaders of this country have with the idea of Somali national unity.

In sum, colonization has not diminished the idea of the unity of a Somali nation, rather it has brought in a new concept, that of a "Somali Union", which will be conceptualized under the indigenous term "soomaalinimo".

Somali Union or Soomaalinimo: An Offspring Concept of the Colonization Period

The term Soomaalinimo is a pure product of the Somali intelligentsia of the colonial period. It can be translated in different ways, depending on the ideological content assigned to it: somalihood (Mohamed D. Afrah[87]), somaliness (cf. Suzanne Lilius, 2001), or somalinism. The latter indicates more the ideological and political content of the concept, whereas the two other denominations are associated with ethnicity or a general code of conduct related to Somali culture. The polysemy and ambiguity of the word "soomaalinimo" obscures, until today, the Somali Union. In fact the very essence of this project is "soomaali-midnimo" or more precisely "midnimo Soomaaliyeed", which should not be translated as the "Unity of Somali people" but rather as "Somali Union".

Martina Steiner (2001:199)[88] who analysed the term "Somaliness", differentiates an "emic" significance which refers more to the "self-identification" or the self-representation as a person belonging to a particular group and an "etic" perspective which "refers to the non-Somalis's view on Somaliness".During the colonial period when the great majority of Somalis were engaged against colonialism and looked for their political union, it was indeed the "etic" meaning of Soomaalinimo which was prevailing. The word was used to assert against "others" (especially occupying powers or competing ethnic groups) the unity of the five divided Somali regions.

But, we wonder if the word "soomaalinimo" has still this latter meaning in people's minds, since the project of "Great Somalia" is no longer on the agenda for the establishment of a singular Somali territory. Even in the new constitution of the FSS, drafted on 2012, the Somali Union project has been dropped out. Thus the term "soomaalinimo" has more an emic connotation which opposes those who are engaged in rebuilding the destroyed central state in Moqadisho from those defending regional or autonomous entities.

The change in the scope of the word "soomaalinimo", the central concept of unification, is soundly linked to the political change which occurred in the Horn of Africa, from the end of 1980s onwards and constituted another major event which has ruined the concept of the Somali Union, as had been envisioned from the beginning of 20th century. In fact, it is only in the former Italian Somalia that this term has kept its effectiveness and operational meaning. If we consider the four other parts of Somali territory, it seems that "soomaalinimo" has no longer its former political mobilization effect, as it had during the colonization period, even if every individual Somali claims his somalihood/somaliness. The tables below can help us to grasp this shift and the evolution of the "soomaalinimo" concept throughout the Somali territories and the period under consideration.

To understand better the difference[89] of the impact of the concept in the various Somali territories, we need to take into account the following criteria : a) The political status of the territory, b) The ethnic diversity in the territory, c) The size of Somali group vs other ethnic groups of the territory; d) The clan diversity within Somali group in the territory, e) The attitude about "Soomaalinimo" (Somalinism), f) the attitude about the SUPP.

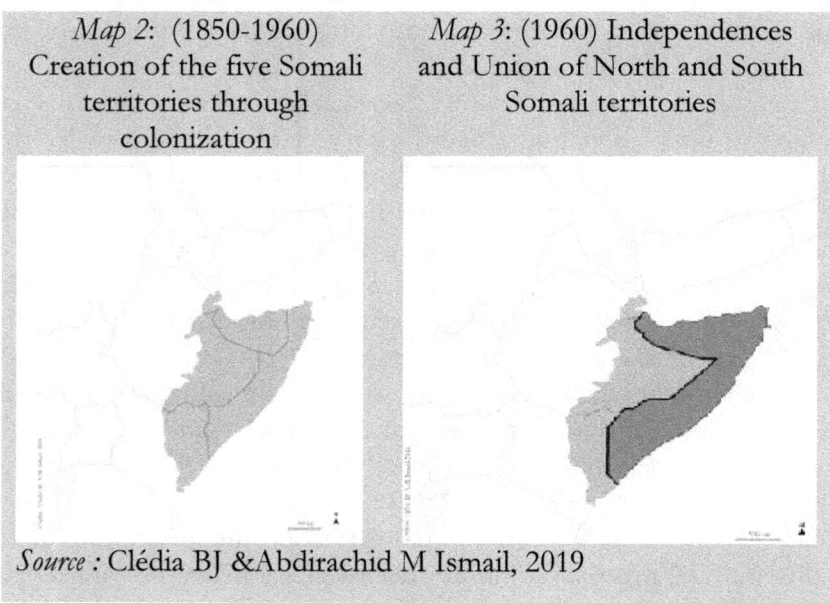

Map 2: (1850-1960) Creation of the five Somali territories through colonization

Map 3: (1960) Independences and Union of North and South Somali territories

Source : Clédia BJ &Abdirachid M Ismail, 2019

Table 2: The perception of *Soomalinomo* concept in the five Somali territories, 1950-1960.

	(A) Political Situation Of The Territory	(B) Ethnic Diversity	(C) Somalis/ Other Ethnic Groups	(D) Clan[90]Diversity	(E) Soomaalinimo Concept Impact	(F) Somali Union Political Project	Score
CFS[91]-Djibouti	Dominated	Relative Heterogeneity	Majority	Relative Homogeneity	Empowering	On The Agenda	4
NFD-Kenya[92]	Dominated	Relative Heterogeneity	Minority	Relative Heterogeneity	Empowering	On The Agenda	2
WST-E[93]	Dominated	Relative Heterogeneity	Minority	Relative Heterogeneity	Empowering	On The Agenda	2
Bristish Somaliland	Towards Sovereignty	Relative Homogeneity	Majority	Relative Homogeneity	Empowering	On The Agenda	5
Italian Somaliland	Towards Sovereignty	Relative Homogeneity	Majority	Relative Heterogeneity	Empowering	On The Agenda	4
TOTAL	Somali Nation General Situation						17

The word in bold indicates the score 1 and the non-bold word indicates the score 0. The first criteria is about the political situation of the territories which varies, during the time, from dominated (score 0) to independence and becoming the recognized state (score 1), with different variations in-between which are not taken into account here. b) The second criteria refers to the ethnic homogeneity/rel. homogeneity (score 1) or heterogeneity/rel. heterogeneity (score 0) of the territory. We have considered a territory relatively homogeneous if the great majority of the inhabitants are genealogically related to Somalis. c) The ratio of the Somali groups living in the country and the other ethnic groups with whom they live, is also significant. If the Somalis are the majority group (score 1) or a minority group (0), they will not have the same attitude towards the concept of "Soomaalinimo" and the SUPP. The Somalis living with other ethnic groups will develop different strategies and attitudes to reach their own goals[94] than those who are living in an ethnically Somali homogeneous territory. d) The attitude about "soomaalinimo" can be perceived through the speeches of political or social leaders and in the newspapers of the territory. e) The last criterion is the official commitment to the Somali Union project which can be grasped through public policy and the explicit reference to the "Somali Union project". f) This is an important criterion which helps to understand the variation of the frequency of the concept of "Soomaalinimo" as well as the usage of it across Somali territories. It is noticeable that where there is "clan heterogeneity", the concept will acquire more importance and will be used more frequently than in a "clan homogeneity" context. It will serve as a "clan unification factor" which reminds us of the ideological basis of the SUPP.

Table 3: The perception of *Soomalinomo* concept in the five Somali territories, 1960-1975.

	(a) Political Situation Of The Territory	(b) Ethnic Diversity	(c) Somalis/ Other Ethnic Groups	(d) Clan Diversity	(e) Soomaalinimo Concept Impact	(f) Somali Union Political Project	Score
TFAI Djibouti	*Dominated*	*Relative Heterogeneity*	*Majority*	*Relative Homogeneity*	*Empowering*	*On The Agenda*	4
NFD-Kenya	*Dominated*	*Relative Heterogeneity*	*Minority*	*Relative Heterogeneity*	*Empowering*	*On The Agenda*	2
WST-Ethiopia	*Dominated*	*Relative Heterogeneity*	*Minority*	*Relative Heterogeneity*	*Empowering*	*On The Agenda*	2
Somalia Republic	*Independent*	*Relative Homogeneity*	*Majority*	*Heterogeneity*	*Empowering*	*On The Agenda*	10
TOTAL	Somali Nation General Situation						18

The total score of "Somalia Republic" is doubled, since it represents the addition of the score of the two former territories which constituted this Republic. This is the best period for the SUPP as Laitin and Samatar (Ibid.:151) have described it: "British Somaliland and Italian Somalia achieved independence in 1960 in a wave of optimism. Two of the Somalilands were united. The possibility of bringing the NFD, French Somaliland and the Ogadeen into the fold appeared good. Somali leaders wished to pursue that goal of a united Somalia."

Table 4: The Perception of *Soomalinomo* Concept in the Five Somali Territories, 1980-1991.

	(a) Political Situation Of The Territory	(b) Ethnic Diversity	(c) Somalis/ Other Ethnic Groups	(d) Clan Diversity	(e) Soomaalinimo Concept Impact	(f) Somali Union Political Project	Score
TFAI Djibouti	*Recognized State*	*Relative Heterogeneity*	*Majority*	*Relative Homogeneity*	*Weak*	*Not On The Agenda*	3
NFD-Kenya	*Dominated*	*Relative. Heterogeneity*	*Minority*	*Relative Heterogeneity*	*Weak (?)*	*Not On The Agenda*	1 (?)
WST-Ethiopia	*Dominated*	*Relative Heterogeneity*	*Minority*	*Relative Heterogeneity*	*Weak*	*Not On The Agenda*	0
Somalia Republic	*Unstable Civil War*	*Relative Homogeneity*	*Majority*	*Heterogeneity*	*Weak*	*Ambiguous*	4
TOTAL	Somali Nation General Situation						7 To 8

This period is the turning point for the SUPP since it corresponds to the collapse of the central government of Somalia and the beginning of the civil war. The SUPP comes to a final standstill and the ideal of soomaalimo is in its worst phase from its first use as a political program. However, from the 1995, the Ethiopian federal constitution and the establishment of functional regional Somali states within the former Republic of Somalia, the Somali nation entered into a new area of its history. It is the most incredible and paradoxical outcome of the entire reorganization of the Horn of Africa. In fact, from that period, there is a progressive and general economic improvement of the Somali populations[95] on one hand, and on the other, the general deterioration of Somali national political influence within the Horn of Africa. Indeed, the period 1992-2012 was the most painful period that Somali nation has ever gone through. And what is particularly remarkable is that during this period, Somalis were struggling between themselves with no external enemy.

Table 5: The Perception of *Soomalinomo* Concept in the Five Somali Territories, Jan. 2019.

	(a) Political Situation of the territory	(b) Ethnic diversity	(c) Somalis/ other ethnic groups	(d) Clan diversity	(e) Soomaalinimo concept impact	(f) Somali Union Political Project	score
Djibouti	*Recognized State*	*Relative Heterogeneity*	*Majority*	*Relative Homogeneity*	*Medium-strong*	*No longer on the agenda*	3-4
NE-Kenya (NEK)	*Decentralized Counties*	*Relative Heterogeneity*	*Minority*	*Relative Heterogeneity*	*Medium-strong*	*No longer on the agenda*	1-2
Somali Region of Ethiopia (SRE)	*Decentralized region*	*Relative Heterogeneity*	*Minority*	*Relative Heterogeneity*	*Medium-strong*	*No longer on the agenda*	1-2
Somaliland	*Unrecognized State*	*Homogeneous*	*Majority*	*Relative Homogeneity*	*Weak*	*No longer on the agenda*	3
Somalia	*Federal State*	*Relative Homogeneity*	*Majority*	*Relative Heterogeneity*	*Strong*	*No longer on the agenda*	4
TOTAL	Somali nation general situation						12-15

A few remarks: The criteria (b to e) are stable in every territory. They illustrate the demographic reality of each territory which did not change during the period under analysis. The other criteria are improvable for every territory. Let's examine how this can be achieved.

The Political Situation of the Territory

The score for this criteria is difficult to improve for at least three territories (Djibouti, SRE and NEK), for different reasons. Djibouti is already an independent country and being a multi-ethnic country, its policy is based on the unity of its ethnic components and even if it supports state building of Somalia, this is not interpretable as a commitment to the post-independence SUPP. From Djibouti's point view, Somali Unity Political Project is consistent for application in the regions of the former Republic of Somalia.

The SRE and NEK are not independent regions, but, since the Nineties, these regions have undergone important changes, which lead them to be more integrated economically and politically into the countries they are part of today. Because of this process of integration, their commitment to SUPP is outdated. It seems that they are more concerned with being recognized within the countries they are part of today than that of the central State of Somalia central state. "Soomaalinimo" is no longer empowering for them as it used to be in the 50s-70s.

The case of Somaliland is slightly different since it is a mono-ethnic territory which is ideally favorable for soomaalinimo. But this territory seems to be the one on which the idea of "soomaalinimo" has the weakest impact. Here our analysis comes to a paradox. We have supposed that the independence of a Somali territory was the first step of the SUPP and such territory has a score 1. However, in the case of Somaliland, this seems to be the reverse. The self-declaration of independence from the FSS seems to have weakened the soomaalinimo impact on Somaliland. This leads to a contradiction which needs to be solved. In fact, the impact of soomaalinimo political meaning may be weak in Somaliland because it is felt that this idea of soomaalinimo is like a hook to get it back into the fold of previous Somalian regimes, a pitfall to put it back to the same system which has failed. Another point which needs to be considered and which seems to be contradictory, is the fact that for Djibouti, SRE and NEK populations, the SUPP is no longer in their agenda, but the impact of Soomaalinimo concept is perceived as "medium to strong". The growing exchange and contacts between the populations of Somali territories seem to have led to the weakening of the SUPP political dimension.

The Federal State of Somalia seems to have a strong commitment to "soomaalinimo", but this has nothing to do with the concept of the 1960s or 1970s. At that time, the soomaalinimo was an externally oriented concept, to unite with the other three territories identified within the SUPP. Today, it has an internally oriented meaning which aims to maintain the different regions together, which regions are strong regional-clan states, some of them anterior to the creation of the federal state itself (Somaliland, Puntland, South-West State). The FSS has no other political project of maintaining the internal unity but stressing the political key-concept of soomaalinimo, which is the common denominator between the clans and the simplest and most efficient tool to mobilize for this unity, even if the original ideological background has gradually lost its relevance. The SUPP, as it was conceived from the beginning of the 20th century, is in fact dead because almost no Somali territory has any agenda to achieve the same at the concurrent times. The extradition of Abdikarim Sheick Muuse, known as "Qalbi Dhagax", on the 28th August 2017 to the federal State of Ethiopia, was in itself a proof that the FSS has no longer a claim on the Western Somali territory and that the dispute over this territory with the Ethiopians has been settled.

The question is now why the SUPP has failed to fully move forward.

Understanding SUPP to Understand Somalia recent History

No clannism, no dictatorship, no nepotism, no corruption, or external interventions have been the real cause of Somalian collapse, as it is often reported.[96] All these flaws are only symptoms which are the outcomes of a state building program based on the SUPP, which, in every aspect was actually condemned to death from birth. Saving this project was highly improbable for several reasons. One of them being the fact that those who had conceived it, and were the only ones who could do so, were not those who had the legitimacy and the skills to fulfill it, namely the intellectual elites.

The SUPP, which has monopolized our attention during decades, especially during the pre-independence period, has not permitted sufficient reflection on formulation of the national state in the Somali context. The SUPP was based on a centralized conception of state building which was at the antipodes of Somali traditional mode of political organization formulation (this organization was labelled by Lewis as "pastoral democracy" or by Michael Notten[97] as "Kritarchy").This centralized conception was first promoted by Sayid Mohamed 'Abdalla Hassan who tried to mobilize Somalis around the concept of Soomaalinimo, against the colonizers.

Putting aside the theological divergence between the different religious orders, the Somalis had not experienced a trans-tribal mode of governance or election, except that of the western countries[98]. The legitimacy of the Chief in a clan or tribe was based on known rules within each clan, but the unification of the clans under a unique patron was something new which had neither been discussed nor experimented ever.

The Dervish movement was not destroyed by the British but because of insufficient support from Somalis who had not adhered to the centralized trans-tribal power of the Sayid. And he, while calling for unification based on soomaalinimo, was still using clan terminology, mode of thinking and pastoral practices of raids and revenge.

After the Dervish movement, the intellectual elites, who were in contact with the westerners or with the Islamic world, through travelling and religious orders, were the first to promote the SUPP. Lewis[99] describes that from the 1920s and especially during the decade between the 30s and 40s, growing Somali nationalism was indeed based on what we have called SUPP. He says:

> ...with the traditional Somali national consciousness, which the experiences of Italian patriotic fervor presented in a new light and the long suppressed reaction to alien rule, all combined to provide conditions favorable to the emergence of new aspirations. Thus, in the last few years of the short lived Italian East African Empire, the first definite steps towards the creation of a modern nationalist movement began to be taken in Somalia. These took the form of small clandestine meetings, organized mainly, it appears, by some of the new generations of Somalis who had been to school and were employed by the Italian government.[100]

In the north, it was also the same social class who were sensitive to the SUPP and the liberation from colonial powers: "Again, the first impetus seems to have come from the few Somalis who, after education in Aden or the Sudan, had returned to find employment in the clerical grades of the civil service. One of the earliest of these to espouse the new aspirations and to seek to promote the general social and political betterment of his countrymen was Haji Farah Omar, a former employee of the Administration, who became active in the 1920s."[101]

From these beginnings, we see the SUPP coming up progressively from the vision of Somali elites who were strongly influenced by foreign conceptions of State building. In Lewis's description, we could view very neatly the SUPP settlement: "From these tentative beginnings the Somaliland National Society emerged shortly afterwards. Its principal aims were to encourage modern education and progress in general and to seek to overcome the traditional, particularistic rivalries which divided Somali society." After that, another prominent Somali organization was created in Mogadiscio on March 1943, the Somali Youth Club, the ancestor of the Somali Youth League (SYL), the most famous and powerful pan-Somalist organization, composed of members from the main Somali clans and "united in the desire to abolish the wasteful clan rivalries of the past and to establish a new conception of nationhood".[102]

At last, the SUPP was formalized in 1959 in Mogadisho by the gathering of all Somali parties to form the National Pan-Somali Movement with the main aim of campaigning " for the independence and unification of all the Somali territories" (Lewis, ibid.)

The tragic situation which was associated with this event was that there was almost no other alternative which could be approved by the majority of Somalis. The independence and unification of all Somali territories was the obvious and natural plan which was conceivable by everyone, irrespective of his/her class and the region he/she belonged to. The greatness and empowering impact of the project which infuses strength and considerable hope of betterment have veiled the difficulty to implement it, regarding traditional and inherent Somali policy structure. It was like putting a square peg in a round hole... in fact they did not even try to put it in the round hole, until the political independence of British Somaliland and Italia Somalia became a reality. At that moment, they had to face reality and implement their borrowed ideology based on a highly centralized state which banishes any clan reference or particularism. For about nine years, they tried hard and struggled, with every kind of possible contortion, to realize this aim. But all scholars have observed "the re-emergence of clan interests and clan politics reached a peak in the 1969, coinciding with the general elections. One hundred and twenty-six "clanistic" political groups competed, each one hoping to gain more power for itself" (M-R Sheik Hassan, 1993:198).[103]

Ibrahim Moallin Mursal (2001) also assigns liability of Somali State failure in 1991 to the imported system of governance which had been corrupted with indigenous elements (sic):

> The Somalia Republic...was born as a State of Law, *Stato di Dirrito*; organized and shaped in the form of a western-style cultural system. To accommodate this system with the social and traditional need of the Somali population, exceptions and special cases were introduced to the extent that it overwhelmed the rule of law and thus, aroused personal greed.[104]

Even at that stage, the first part of the proposition "a State of law...organized and shaped in the form of a western-style cultural system" had not been put into a question. So, it was not only hard to reconsider the SUPP and the principles on which it was built, but it was much harder to conceive a state built on indigenous rules. There was a common vision among African politicians and intellectuals of the post-independence period that the traditional and indigenous mode of organization was primitive and inadequate compared to the modern world and should be cast out. As Omar Osman Rabeh[105] was still putting it in 1985, African societies have to "cast away its old skin, make a new one, catch time it needs to pass from one phase of its existence to another."

In this condition, considerations like those mentioned by Marleen Renders (2007)[106] or by Michael Notton (2003)[107] about "traditional political system", would have been at least inaudible and most thoroughly condemned as an outdated ugly duckling.

What was the alpha and omega of the military coup of 1969? To reinforce the SUPP which seemed to be in danger and impose with more strength and coercion a centralized power in the most decentralized society. The tool to realize this aim had been to import a marxism-leninism based ideology, which was born in a pre-industrial context, far way of the mostly rural and nomadic or semi-nomadic Somali society. What is obvious, from this perspective, is that Somali society was henceforth running at a pace which was faster its natural constitution. Siyad Barre had become naturally an absolute sultan, being the general secretary of the Revolutionary Socialist Party, the only authorized party, the head of the army, the state security court and judiciary, the president of the country, "with the power to appoint and dismiss high ranking officials.[108]" In fact, he became the Sultan of Somali clans, but without the legitimacy given by clan laws!

The great majority of Somalis during all the 20th century believed and supported the SUPP, as it was conceived from its beginnings at the end of 19th and the early 20th century. Siyad Barre led this project to its ultimate consequences. So many still think that Siyad Barre was misguided about the SUPP, introducing clannism, nepotism, etc and "destroyed most of the ideals the Somali people stood for" (M.-R. Sheikh Hassan, 1993, quoting Abdulgadir Shire Farah, 1990, "Xeebti Geerida").

However, Siyad was only the last offspring of a project which was an ideological mushroom which reveled itself to be poisonous for Somalis.

Somalis have always blamed and still blame "tribalism and clannism", which is their secular and traditional mode of organization and try hard to change it for a western mode of organization based on multipartism. As parties had become tribalized, Siyad had been logical enough to ban all parties, as clans had been banned from politics[109,] to achieve the SUPP goals. Siyad was again logical enough to choose the Social-Marxist system of governance as a model, which was the most centralized power and administrative framework and could fit with the SUPP aims, as he conceived it.

The last logical step of Siyad Barre's action was to impose his rules to fulfill his political program, as does every head of a legitimately recongised State. His dictatorship was the logical and ultimate consequence of an ideology which had begun with Sayid Mohamed Abdalla Hassan and ended with the lost war against Ethiopia in 1977-1978.

The main common point with all dictatorships is to uproot the secular systems which have counter power institutions, to centralize all the powers in one hand. In the case of Siyad Barre, this process was rather natural, since the great majority of Somalis agreed with him to condemn or discredit their secular Somali system of governance as well as the multiparty system. It was why his coup had initially been greeted by the Somali people (Lewis, 1987:210) and many have indeed praised his economic and social realizations during the first years of his governance.

It is worth noticing that Siyad Barre had tried to heal the outcome of ill-governance of the post-independence period, during which governance was based on abstract democratic rules imported from western countries (Lee Cassanelli, 2009:6)[110]. Siyad had not changed this, he had just thought that a more centralized power structure was able to heal the problems of the Somalis and thus imported his "scientific socialism"... The two options lamentably failed, because they used transplant systems without roots in Somali context.

What has been tragic in the Somali case is that there was almost no other option than the SUPP to oppose the colonial rule at that time. It was the ready program, the turn key solution offered by intellectual elites, easily understandable by everyone and empowering all Somalis whatever their regions and clans. This program has not worked because it was ill-adapted to the context of Somali traditions.

On the other hand, there were also other events which seem to have inexorably led to the collapse of the State of Somalia. There had been precisely these "particular incidents".

3. Inexorable Events towards SUPP Failure

The Dervish Turmoil

The first event which can be noted is the increase of contacts with the Arabic peninsula from where "intellectual currents of religious reform from the wider Islamic world had reached the literate Muslims in the coastal towns of Somalia" (Lee Cassanelli, 2009:8)[111]. As this author analyses the process which brought literate Muslims who traveled in the Islamic world for pilgrimage or education to "re-imagine Somalis under the same Islamic rule of the Umma.

There were deep-rooted "versions of Somali solidarity in an Islamic framework" diffused by Sufi orders, in the north as well as in the south of the Somalilands. But, at the end of 19th and early 20th century, the most visible and fiercest opponent to the colonial domination seems to be Sayid Mohamed Abdalla Hasan (according to the available historical records) who at the same time considered those Sufi orders as infidels. This is the reason why he "begun his jihaad in 1899 with a raid on a Qadiriyyeh Sufi zawiya at Sheikh.[112]"

In any case, Sayid Mohamed Abdallah Hassan did not consider either Somali clan organizations or their local and secular spiritual organizations to entertain their Islamic faith. His objective was to unite all his fellow countrymen in war against the colonizing forces under one flag, the one of Islam... Unfortunately, he had not convinced his first opponents in Berbera who were mostly from Qadiriya tariqa. The Sayid project was immense but based neither on traditional *xeer* nor on an Islamic law accepted by the majority of the Somalis. And his prodigious oratory talent and extraordinary strength and vigor were not enough to fill the gap. Even so, he has left a strong legacy of anti-colonialism to lighten the grip of colonial administrations who would be haunted by the thought that the "specter of another 'Mad Mulla' rises in Somalilands" (Geshekter, *ibid* : 235).

The First International Statement against SUPP

After the Second World War, it was decided to deprive Italy of all its colonies, among them its African colonies (Eritrea, Libya, Cyrenaica and Somalia) at the Paris Conference on 29th july-15th October 1946. At that time, the British were occupying four Somali territories (British Somaliland, Italia Somalia, and NFD in Kenya, Socotra Island) and seemed favorable to unite all Somalis territories. That was at least the essence of Ernest Bevin's proposal, representing the UK Ministry of Foreign Affairs at that time, to the British House of Parliament on 4th June 1946.

But for many reasons, this proposal was not implemented; probably the British had not been deeply involved in Bevin's plan, the Soviet Union and USA may have been suspicious of leaving to the British so large a territory to administer as a protectorate until independence; indeed the French, who were already occupying the French Somali Coast, were more than reluctant to this proposition, and Ethiopia was lobbying to get its part from Italy's possessions, especially the Western Somali territory. Ambassador Mohamed Omar Osman (2006:136) explains with details how the hope for greater Somalia was killed again when "The Paris Peace Conference...decided to discuss only the Italian Somalia and completely ignored other Somali territories which were languishing under colonial rule."

Ogaden and Hawd Handed over to Ethiopia

It was one of the most heart-breaking events which preceded the independence of the first Somali territory and indeed one of the most poisonous seed planted among Somalis. After having conceded to Ethiopia, in 1897, "the most fertile grain producing regions in the west of the Protectorate (The British Somaliland Protectorate) and the important spring and autumn pastures in the South[113]", again, after the brief Italian occupation, the British government gave back to Ethiopia the Ogaden region on 1948 and the Haud and the Reserved Area on 1954. Menelik's reign had been one of the most brutal forms of colonization that Somalis had ever experienced and the abandonment of these territories to Ethiopia seemed to them "*sida middi dhabarka lagaaga dhuftoo kalé*", since it was a betrayal of the former treaties of 1884 and

1886 between the Somalis and the British (cf. Mohamed Osman, 2006: 82)[114].

In the 20th century, Ethiopia "represented the consolidation, expansion and transformation of a feudal-military principality (Abyssinia) into a veritable multi-ethnic African empire-state"[115], "the only African state below the Sahara whose boundaries have been determined by induced process of expansion."[116](Geshekter, 1986:222)

As a consequence, Somalis have been the only African nation colonized by another African independent country whereas the European colonization was comming to a close. Because of that, "nowhere have the consequences of African adjustment to the postcolonial age been more destructive than in the Horn of Africa where Ethiopia and Somalia have waged fratricidal war to determine whether the Ogaden should be part of Ethiopia or become a Somali territory." (Geshekter, Ibid: 217)

This historical injustice, following the International biased solution which had singled out the Italian colony to be prepared for independence, ignoring the other Somali territories under colonial rule, could not be assigned to any Somali responsability. Yet, it is part of these "incidental events" which led to the collapse of the Somali State on 1991. Even when the Bristish government was manoeuvring to abandon these territories to Ethiopia, it was not meant to plant chaos among Somalis. Its main objective was essentially a matter to counterbalance the solid relations of the French State with Ethiopia and to have a good relation with the latter which had an important border with Kenya British Protectorate.

The Abandon of the NFD to Kenya

Again the SUPP would meet with misfortune when the NFD of Kenya was abandoned to Kenya on March 1963, whereas its Somali population, composing the majority of the district, "almost unanimously" voted for secession from Kenya and were favorable to join the Republic of Somalia.

This territory was not challenged aggressively between Somalia and Kenya for years before this decision, as Lewis is asserting here:

> For several years prior to the 1962 Kenya conference, the Provincial Administration of the NFD had consistenty reported on the direction

and strength of Somali feeling. Had these reports received serious attention, it would clearly have been possible for the British government to have prepared the ground for the eventual secession of the NFD without, at that stage, incurring serious opposition from African opinion in Kenya...was left until it become insoluble except at the cost of alienating one side or the other.[117]

Indeed, Somalis had not received any support from the other African leaders on this issue, despite the Somali government promoting the complementarity of Pan-Africanism and Pan-Somalinism. But in fact, the two ideas were not so complementary, since pan-Somalinism was accused to run "counter the unification in other African states"[118], at least two of them.

Others Events Upsetting SUPP

Among other events, there was also a most conspicuous event happening before the collapse of the State of Somalia in the 1977-78 war against Ethiopia. Contrary to what is often reported, one of the main protagonist of this event, General Maxamad Nuur Galaal, states that this war had been suggested first by the Soviet Union to Somali leaders of that time and materially supported by communist countries. He says that "when the Soviet Union lost its military base in Egypt, after Anwar Saddad swung in Unites States' favour, they decided to take revenge over him...and to move off the Americans from the Saudi Arabia and the Arabic Peninsula."[119] It was in 1974 and Haile Selassie was still in power. The idea was to overthrow the monarchy and replace it with a Marxist state.

Once again things turned to the detriment of the Somalis when, a few months later, Haile Selassie was driven out of power. It took about one or two years before the new Ethiopian leader established his Socialist-Marxist system and gave confidence to the Socialist block. After this change, the Soviet Union, too, changed its strategy and tried, indirectly, through other communist powers, such as Cuba or northern Yemen, to persuade Somalia to stop the guerilla organisation it was steering from 1975 against Ethiopia in the Ogaden region. The proposals of these states were totally unrealistic since they suggested to the Somalian leader the idea of forming a federal socialist state of the horn of Africa, with Ethiopia, Eritrea and Sudan; Djibouti was not yet independent. Again, there was almost no other alternative, except to postpone the SUPP. But the project, regarding its first phase, focused on Western Somali territory and was activated from 1974 onwards and was in good progress. To postpone it would have led to great political and strategic damage.

In fact, with the civil war and the fall of monarchy, Ethiopia was going through a very troubled phase which weakened its military response against Somalia supported secessionist groups. But the overthrow of the millennial Ethiopian monarchy by a Socialist regime heavily supported by the Soviet Union and Cuba, counteracted and stopped at the last minute the liberation of the Western Somali territory (WST).

A few years later, almost the same situation happened again. On 3rd April 1988, Somalia and Ethiopia signed an agreement under the auspices of the first president of Djibouti, Hassan Gouled Aptidon. The two countries, both experiencing strong military opposition, were willing to calm down their antagonism[120]. This agreement permitted the two countries to reestablish their diplomatic relations and both accepted not to support any military opposition against each other. The resolution of the question of the western region was referred to future negotiations.

In the meantime the two regimes collapsed at the same time. Siyad Barre was removed from power on 27th January 1991 and Mengistu Haile Mariam, a few months later, on May 21st, 1991, almost for the same reason: a heavily centralized and autocratic power. Again, what would save Ethiopia from destruction had not been imagined by Somali leaders for Somalia. Ethiopia adopted maximum decentralization, to the extent that any nation under Ethiopian sovereignty was given the right to "self-determination". Because of that, Meles Zenawi was able to draw up the "new Ethiopia" and turn Ethiopia's ethnic diversity, which had seemed to be a true handicap for national unity, into a formidable opportunity. In opposition, it seems that Somali political leaders have been incapable of taking advantage of the Somali ethnic unity to turn it into an effective opportunity. We will come back to this point.

Just let's notice, for now, that when Ethiopia came to a standstill after the overthrow of the Socialist regime, there was no longer a Somali state to claim the WST.

Because the SUPP had failed ostensibly and the central State of Somalia had collapsed, the Western Somali Territory of Ethiopia decided to stay within the new federal state of Ethiopia, even if the principle of self-determination had been given to every Ethiopian nation.

The following logical and final step came later with the provisional federal constitution of Somalia (adopted on 1st August 2012) which had suppressed the Article 6.4 of the 1963 constitution of Somalia, which stated this: "The Somali Republic shall promote, by legal and peaceful means, the union of Somali territories and encourage solidarity among the peoples of the world and in particular among African and Islamic peoples." This meant that Somalia had ceased its claim over the Somali territories under foreign rule and consequently the SUPP, such as it was conceived at the beginning of the 21st century, had officially come to an end.

4. Conclusion

First, the Somali Central state collapsed in 1991, not because Siyad Barre's regime had failed, but because he had led to the ultimate consequences of a political project which had failed since Sayid Mohamed Abdallah Hassan. The latter was the first who had not been able to mobilize all Somalis around this project, which was in fact the Somali Union Political Project (SUPP). The historicization of the SUPP, built around a cheerful romanticization of the Dervish movement,[121] had obscured the real reasons of its failure and had consequently misled those who have followed in its steps, meaning most of the nationalist movements, until the late Mohamed Siyad Barre and the current political and religious leaders.

Second, whatever the capacity or incapacity[122] of Somali political actors of almost one century could be, this failure is strongly linked to the real nature of the SUPP, which was insufficiently defined and based, from the origin, on overseas models of state governments.

During almost one century, Somalis have tried to "unite" themselves by getting rid of themselves, by struggling with the western colonialists while at the same time holding their system as the ideal reference. They have been caught by James Ferguson's "shadow"[123] which makes Africans attached to western systems and explains in some ways their underdevelopment.

So, Somalis have battled with themselves to jump across the gap between their traditional model of organization and the idealized western system of governance. That led them to an "idealistic" abstract state which gave rise to the "invention of Somalia". Every political leading candidate has been promising that Somalis will do the great jump and realize the SUPP goals and sine qua non condition for that has been to banish the pillar of their secular political organization. But "what's bred in the bone will come out in the flesh". The leaders have not paid attention to the Somali proverb that says *"midho dhabta kuugu jira loo ma daadiyo kuwo geed saran"* (i.e "a bird in the hand is worth two in the bush"). As Abdalla O. Mansur confirms: "The present Somali clan system has lost its traditional xeer ("customary law"), [and as a consequence]...we are, as they say, neither fish nor fowl, neither clans nor state" (Abdalla Mansur, 1995:115)[124].

In addition, we have tried to show that there is not only an insufficient or biased definition of the SUPP which has caused the present situation of the Somali nation but also a constant flow of interwoven events which have frustrated the realization of SUPP as it was conceived and still is by most of the prominent Somali intellectuals.

What is happening now, in front of our eyes, with the building of the Federal State of Somalia and the global situation of the Somali nation, testifies to the end of the original format of SUPP. Somali State reconstruction is today comparable to a river current which has been blocked for decades and is now taking its natural state, after having overflowed the obstacle.

That leads us finally to the question: Does the Somali unity project have to be thrown away into the trash bin of history? We believe no! Simply because it is a natural tendency that "what belongs together comes together" and that does not go against any international law.

In the second part, we will present some ideas to assist in the progression towards this natural state.

References

[45] Ahmed I. Samatar (2001), "The somali Catastrophe, Explanations and Implications", In *Variations on the theme of Somaliness",* Ed. by Muddle

Suzanne Lilius, Proceedings of the EASS/SSIA congress, 1998, Turku, Abo Akademi University.
46 Ali Jimale Ahmed (2001), "The three blind men and the elephant. In search of a holistic view of Somalia.A comment to Ahmed I. Samatar", In *Variations on the theme of Somaliness"*, Ed. by Muddle Suzanne Lilius.
47 Omar Osman Rabeh (1985), *The Somali nation, III : the state and society, theorical considerations*, Paris : Seecop.
48 Omar Osman Rabeh (1985), *id*: 12.
49 Translated from *Le phénomène Humain* (1970), Ed. Le Seuil, Paris.
50 Watzlawick Paul (1984), *The invented reality*, Ed. Paul Watzlawick, Penguins Books Canada.
51 von Glasersfeld Ernst (1988), "The Reluctance to Change a Way of Thinking," *Irish Journal of Psychology*, 9 (1), 83–90, 1988.
52 Abdisalam M. Issa-Salwe (1993), "The Failure of The Daraawiish State The Clash Between Somali Clanship and State System", https://web.archive.org/web/20040815122806/http://somaliawatch.org/archivemar03/040629602.htm
53 Slight John P. (2011), "British and Somali Views of Muhammad Abdullah Hassan's Jihad, 1899–1920", In *Bildhaan*: An International Journal of Somali Studies: Vol. 10 , Article 7.
54 Cabdiraxmaan C. Faarax, "Barwaqo" (2012), *Sooyaal: Ina CabduleXasan ma Sheekhbuuahaamise*, Hargeisa.
55 Yasiin Cismaan Keenedid (1984), *Ina Cabdille Xasan e la sua attività letteraria*, Ed. Napoli Istituto universitario orientale.
56 Aw Jaamac C. Isse (2005), *Taariikhdii Daraawiishta iyo Diiwaankii Daraawiishta*, 3 Tomes, Re-edited by ILD, Cerd, Djibouti.
57 He says precisely that "It has no movement or development to exhibit. Historical movements in it — that is in its northern part — belong to the Asiatic or European World."
58 *Cf* Omar Osman Rabeh, *ibid.*,p.10.
59 Prebisch Raul (1959), "Commercial policy in the underdeveloped countries", In *American Sociological Review* 49(2): 251–273.
60 Hryniewicz Janusz (2014), "Core-periphery: An Old Theory in New Times", In *European Political Science*, September 2014:2, University of

Warsaw. https://www.researchgate.net/publication/265172869_Core-periphery_An_Old_Theory_in_New_Times

[61] Durkheim Emile (1925), *L'Education morale*, Alcan, p. 183, Paris. http://philosophie.accreteil.fr/IMG/pdf/education_morale.pdf

[62] Catherine WanjikuNyambura (2011), "The multifarious interlinked causes of conflict in Somalia and the way forward", In *Journal of Language, Technology & Entrepreneurship in Africa Vol. 3 No.1.*

[63] *Somalia Clan and State Politics*, ITPCM International Commentary December 2013. https://reliefweb.int/sites/reliefweb.int/files/resources/_COMMENTARY_SOMALIA_ISSUE_DEC_2013.pdf

[64] I would like here to quote among these works the outstanding thesis of LadanAffi (2012) who shows how the Somali Diaspora "has been a neglected but critical actor in the collapse of the Somali state" and its difficult rebuilding. *Cf.* Ladan Affi (2012), *Destroying and Constructing the State from Below: The Role of the Somali Diaspora in Conflict, Development and Governance*, PhD dissertation, University of Wisconsin-Madison.

[65] Catherine Wanjiku Nyambura, *Ibid.*

[66] Abdullahi Mohammed Odow, in his article titled "What can current leaders in Somalia learn from their past history?", he argues "that historically Somalia and its citizens have never had the type of leaders who possessed a balance of vision, competence and power to successfully promote a message of justice, unity and hope." *Somalia Clan and State Politics*, ITPCM International Commentary December 2013. https://reliefweb.int/sites/reliefweb.int/files/resources/_COMMENTARY_SOMALIA_ISSUE_DEC_2013.pdf

[67] Gonnelli Michele (2013), *Somalia Clan and State Politics*, ITPCM International Commentary, December 2013. https://reliefweb.int/sites/reliefweb.int/files/resources/_COMMENTARY_SOMALIA_ISSUE_DEC_2013.pdf

[68] *Idem.*

[69] Title from the Proceedings of the 10th SSIAC, edited by Kadar Ali Diraneh in 2015, Djibouti.

[70] Even if Somaliland is not recognized as an independent country, it has acted as such since 1991. A situation that some foreign countries take advantage of for their

own political and economic interests and can seriously endanger Somali national unity.

[71] Speaking recently to The Associated Press in the capital, Hargeisa, about the agreement that allows the United Arab Emirates to establish a military base in Somaliland, Muse Bihi, President of Somaliland, declared: "*Our government is not so strong and our zone needs to be protected. I think we need a friendly country to have a cooperation with military security, we need it.*" http://abcnews.go.com/International/wireStory/ap-interview-somaliland-president-defends-uae-military-deal-54208331.

[72] The telegraph has called Ahmed Abdi Godane, former head of al-Shabab the "new mad Mulla": *Ahmed Abdi Godane: the new 'Mad Mullah' bent on jihah;* and ironically this head of Al-Shabab was killed with one of the most advanced air-attacks, just as Mohamed Abdalla Hassan was targeted with one of the first bombing air-attack. https://www.telegraph.co.uk/news/worldnews/africaandindianocean/somalia/10341725/Ahmed-Abdi-Godane-the-new-Mad-Mullah-bent-on-jihad.html

[73] Maxamad Xirsi Guleed (2002) has metaphorically and beautifully illustrated this situation in his book *Ragga toodii aragnaye, dumar talo mala gadeyey*. ForfattaresBokmaskin, Stockholm.

[74] Kadar Ali Diraneh (2015), *Yesterday is not behind*, p.18, Djibouti.

[75] Ahmed-BachirMahamoud& Mohamed Ibrahim (2015:136), "Désintégration de l'Etat-Nation Somalien", In *Yesterday is not behind*, write: "Le simulacra nationaliste et pan-somali de l'unité a cessé d'exister [en 1991]."

[76] David D. Laitin and Said S. Samatar (1987), *Somalia: Nation in Search of a State*, Boulder, Colo.: Westview or Gower, London.

[77] For Latin and Said Samatar (1987:11), the name Somali appears in the 15th century but Abdirachid M. Ismail (2017) gives the 12th -13th A.D for that, *cf.* Abdirachid M. Ismail, 2017, "An Ancient Cultural Contact between the Somali Coast and the Arabian Peninsula seen through a Folktale", In Dionisius A. Agius&Alun Williams: Red Sea Publications VI, Brill editions.

[78] Latin and Said Samatar, *op. cit.*

[79] Abdallah O. Mansur (1995), in an incisive pamphlet entitled "the Cancer of Somali State", has written that "the nomadic population, moving into the cities and constituting the new ruling class, kept their

nomadic mentality which became, in my opinion, the major obstacle to the growth of a modern state." He goes even further, asserting that "the most serious problem in Somali society today is that cultural traditions are not compatible with a modern state."

[80] Abdisalam M. Issa-Salwe (1993), *Ibid.*; John P. Slight, 2011, *Ibid.*

[81] Geshekter Charles L. (1986), "Anti-colonialism and Class Formation ; The estern Horn of Africa, 1920-1950", In *Proceedings of the Second International Congress of Somali Studies*, Tome II, Edited by Thomas Labahn, University of Hamburg, August 1-6, 1983.

[82] Lewis Ioan M. (1988), *A Modern History Of Somalia: Nation And State In The Horn Of Africa*, Revised, Updated. Published by Westview Press., London, p. 46.

[83] *Ibid.* p.47.

[84] *Op. cit.* p.47.

[85] Lilius Suzanne (2001), "Multiple Loyalty: Complex Identities in the Horn of Africa", In The*Proceedings of the EASS/SSIA Intertional Congress of Somali Studies*", August 6-9 1998, Edited by Muddle Suzanne Lilius, Turku, Finland.

[86] Muauz GideyAlemu (2015) says that "The French instilled ethnicity into Djibouti politics to postpone independence on grounds of ethno-national conflicts and social disarticulation". *Cf. The geopolitics and human security of the Afar in the post-cold war period*, IN African Journal of Political Science and International Relations, Vol.9(6), pp. 225-253 , June 2015.

[87] Maxamed D. Afrax (1994), "The Mirror of Culture: Somali Dissolution seen through Oral Expression", In *The Somali Challenge: from Catastrophe to renewal*, Ed. Ahmed I. Samatar, Lynne Rienner Puplisher, London.

[88] Martina Steiner (2001), "What is the thing called Somaliness ?", In Muddle Suzanne Lilius, 2001.

[89] The data presented in these tables are not based on statistical studies. However the information in columns a), b), c) and d) are based on objective or official data found in various documents (geographical and anthropological reports such as those of Summer International of Linguistics, national census or national elections reports, mainstream political program of the territory, texts read in

newspapers, etc.) For b) and d) we have adopted a four level scale: "homogeneity, relative homogeneity, relative heterogeneity, heterogeneity". If an ethnic group or a clan is perceived by the great majority of individuals as representing the majority of the inhabitants of a territory, we have considered this territory as "homogeneous or relative homogeneous", otherwise, it is marked "heterogeneous or relative heterogeneous" The term "relative" does not introduce any difference in the scores, it is only meant to give a more accurate information. The information in columns e) and f) are based on the author's personal observation about recent Somalis history and the global mainstreams policies in Somali territories. On the whole, we assume that the data shown in the tables 2 to 5 compare well with predictable outcomes, if a serious statistic study is conducted in the issues presented in these tables.

[90] Many authors have discussed the complexity of this concept which relates to different realities according to the political context. In this article the term clan refers to any Somali lineage, either a "family can" or a "sub-clan", which has a political influence in Somali territories.

[91] Côte Française des Somalis.

[92] Northern Frontier District of Kenya.

[93] Western Somali Territory of Ethiopia.

[94] These goals are consistent with the necessary adaptation to one's environment and with strategies related to minorities groups attitudes confronted to assimilation, integration, separation, or marginalization, as Berry's scheme illustrates (*cf.* Berry, J.W. (1997) "Immigration, Acculturation and Adaptation". Applied Psychology: An International Review 46 (1). P. 5-68; NatalijaKasatkina, 2003, "The Adaptation of Ethnic Minority Groups: Defining the Problem (Case of Lithuania)", *Ethnicity Studies*, Vytautas Magnus University, Kaunas, Lithuania).

[95] There can be some exceptions in Southern regions of Somalia, which are facing important destabilization activities from extremist militias and political instability. But even in this hard environment, the economy of the south is booming.

https://www.theguardian.com/cities/2017/may/15/mogadishu-violence-booming-economy-famine

[96] *Cf.* Mohamed Osman Omar (2002:p. x) asserts for instance that "the corrupt regimes that came to power during the years after independence only created division, malpractices and nepotism which facilitated the military coup led by Mohamed SiadBarre in 1969. The military regime aggravated the problems and deepened the divisions among the people.

[97] Notten Michael (2003), Africa: Rivista trimestrale di studi e documentazione dell'Istituto italiano per l'Africa e l'Oriente, Anno 58, n°2, pp. 147-157.

[98] Lewis Ioan M. (1993), "Although the Somali people had traditionally a strong sense of cultural and linguistic unity, they did not form a single political unit."

[99] Lewis, Ioan M., 1988, *Ibid.*

[100] *Opit.cit.* p.113.

[101] *Opit.cit.* p.114.

[102] *Opit.cit.* p.121.

[103] Mohamed-Rashid Sheikh Hassan (1993), "Somali Unity and Military Rule In Somalia", AnthropologieSomalienne. Actes du IIeColloque des Etudes *Somaliennes* (Besançon - 8/11 octobre 1990), Ed. by Mohamed Abdi Mohamed, Besançon, pp.191-205.

[104] Ibrahim MoallinMursal (2001), "Sahan: Yet a Breakthrough in the Somali Crisis?" In Muddle Suzanne, *Ibid.*

[105] Omar Osman Rabeh, (1985), *Ibid.*

[106] Appropriate 'governance-technology'? – Somali clan elders and institutions in the making of the 'Republic of Somaliland', *Afrika Spectrum* 42 (2007) 3: 439-459.

[107] « From Nation-state to stateless nation : the Somali experience », *Africa,* LVIII, 2, 2003, pp.147-157.

[108] Mohamed Rashid Sheikh Hassan, *Ibid,* p.201.

[109] By Law No. 67- 1st Nov. 1970, Siyad Barre banned 'tribalism' and "key elements of xeer, including tribal land, water and grazing rights, as well as collective responsibility and diya-payment (e.g. blood-money compensation)", cf. Dr Andre Le Sage, report July 2005, Report-

Stateless Justice in Somalia Formal and Informal Rule of Law Initiatives Centre for Humanitarian Dialogue, Geneva.

[110] The Partition of Knowledge in Somali Studies: Reflections on Somalia's Fragmented Intellectual Heritage.

[111] Lee Cassanelli (2009), "The Partition of Knowledge in Somali Studies: Reflections on Somalia's Fragmented Intellectual Heritage", *Bildhaan: An International Journal of Somali Studies* Vol. 9.

[112] Slight, *Ibid.* p:17.

[113] Geshekter (1986), *Ibid.* p:233.

[114] Mohamed Osman (2006), *Somalia: Past and Present*, Somali Publications Pvt. Ltd. Mogadishu, Translated into Somali with the title *Somaaliya: HoreiyoHadda*, p.82.

[115] Geshekter, *Ibid.* p. 222.

[116] Markakis Ayele (1978:30), quoted by Geshekter, 1986, *op. cit.*

[117] Lewis, I. (1988), *Modern History* (1988:194).

[118] Lewis, *Ibid.* : 196.

[119] https://www.youtube.com/watch?v=WhKE8LjJDeM

[120] Edouard Sauvignon (1989), « A propos de l'accord du 3 avril 1988 : le problème de la normalisation des relations entre la Somalie et l'Ethiopie », In *AnnuaireFrançais de Droit International*, Année 1989 35 pp. 217-228.

[121] Abdi I. Samatar (2006), "Faithless Power as Fratricide: Is there an Alternative in Somalia", In *Bildan* n°9: "*Sayyid Mohamed Abdulle Hassan, charged by the demands of the colonial officers to abstain from calling for morning prayers in Berbera and infuriated by the Christianization of Somali orphans, took the lead to rid the country of the colonial scourge. Despite the existence of common values and heritage, it was extraordinarily difficult to mobilize the population for an anti-colonial resistance. In addition, the scarcity of military and material resources, and a non existent communication infrastructure, were major barriers to unified and collective action. Sayyid Mohamed's only instruments that gained the attention of Somali people were Islam and the enormous power of his poetic gifts*"

[122] Abdullahi M. Odowa, (2013), « What can current leaders in Somalia learn from their past history?", in *Somalia Clan and State Politics*, ITPCM International Commentary December 2013.

https://reliefweb.int/sites/reliefweb.int/files/resources/_COMMENTARY_SOMALIA_ISSUE_DEC_2013.pdf

[123] Ferguson, James (2009) *Global Shadows: Africa in the Neoliberal World Order.* Durham: Duke University Press, 2009.

[124] Abdalla O. Mansur (1995), "The Nature of the Somali Clan System" In *The Invention of Somalia,* Ed. by Ali Jimcale Ahmed, The Red Sea Press, New-York.

Part II- The Future in the Present

"Take care of the present and the future will take care of itself[125]"

5. The New Project

The proposed reconstruction of the Somali nation here is not indicative of making war on neighboring states to recapture lost territories, but to put in place the structure that allows this nation to maintain its cultural and linguistic cohesion, to consider its shared destiny as a community and to consolidate stability and peace in the Horn of Africa.

To achieve this natural state, the Somali Union Project should respect at least these four principles:
- a) It should not mean the disunion of any other nation and should not be done against any nation.
- b) It should not need to be recognized by others and should be based on indisputable facts.
- c) It should be in concord with Somali secular traditional laws.
- d) It should be in concord with international laws.

The four principles stated above constitute the basis of the new Somali union project; however, there are also four statements which should be acknowledged. First, we need to recognize the failure of the SUPP and the real reason of that. Second, we need to recognize the strategic importance of this project, not only for Somalis, but also for the stability and development of all the Horn of Africa and even for the entirety of Africa, as we will try to illustrate. Third, Somalis need to work for that purpose, using their natural skills, traditional laws and all their resources.

Fourth, Moqadisho has been, at least since the 1960s, the meeting place, the incubator and the catalyst for the ideal of a Somali Nation. That is why the fate of the Somali State has been intimately interwoven with that of the Somali national union. This union has not been achieved through the SUPP and the Somali central state which promoted it, did not survive the failure of the SUPP. This shows that the Somali national project will live again with Moqadisho or die with it once and for all. And it is not by mere chance that the greatest opposition and violence (map 6) is concentrated in Moqadisho; because it has been for decades and still is the backbone, the central axis, the core-nucleus of any Somali Union Project.

It is why this new project should be carried out principally by the FSS, even if it needs full participation of every Somali clan or sub-clan and Somali political territories.

Purpose and Definition of the Project

This new Somali Union is built on the basis of the experiences acquired from the old one, which was conceived during the colonial period. The international as well as the regional and the Somali contexts of the Horn have changed since the 1990's. It has already been explained that it is a legitimate and natural process for people who have strong ties to come together in one way or the other.

Another reason which justifies this project is the opportunity for the Somali nation to establish the relevant structure, whatever form it may have, which is in concord with their history and secular traditions.

There is harsh competition between the superpowers for African resources in general and at the Horn of Africa in particular. Along the Red Sea and the Indian Ocean the Somalis have more than three thousand kilometers of coastline, one of the longest in Africa. Due to this position, control over Somali territories is most coveted since it is strategic for the international trade as well as for the landlocked countries of Africa such as that of Ethiopia. The Federal state of Somalia, which is weakened by the extremist groups affiliated to Al Qa'ida or the Islamic State is particularly vulnerable. The recent controversy about the relationship of Djibouti and Berbera with the company DP Word is one of the warning signs of the kind of new adversity which is experienced by the Somalis due to the fierce international competitions for resources and geo-strategic positions.

During colonization, Somalis were divided into five parts. Today, not only these five parts are not yet united, but even the central state of Somali Republic has been broken into pieces (cf. map 6). The necessity of today, if the risk of nothing else having been done could come true, is to reinforce the former divisions and create new ones. In maps 5 and 6, we have tried to show that this risk is real since the present map of the Somali nation looks very much like that of the 19th century.

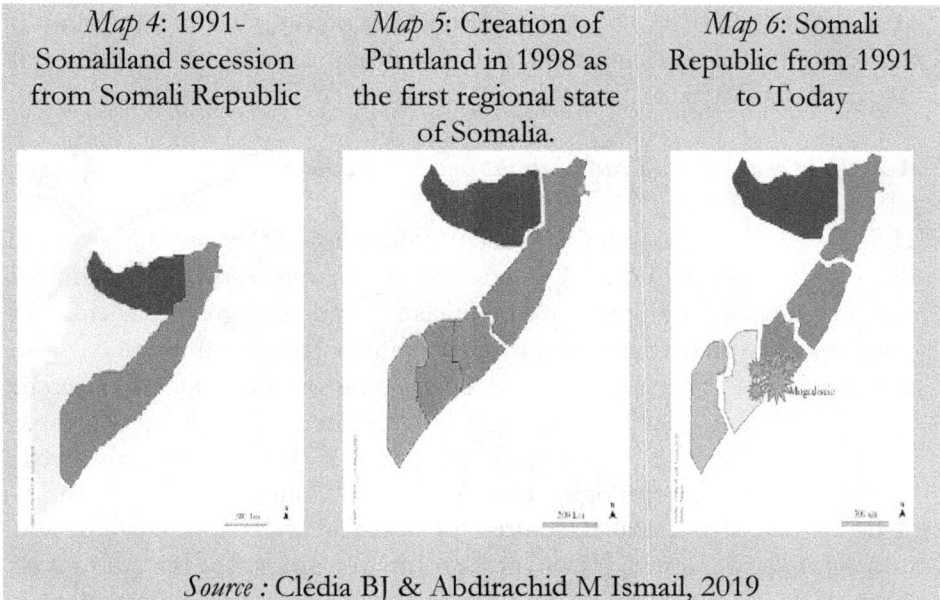

Source : Clédia BJ & Abdirachid M Ismail, 2019

So, the Somali Union Project is not simply natural, but it also is essential for a stable, balanced and peaceful Horn of Africa.

We thus consider that the consolidation of the Somali central state and the building of a Somali National Union should go hand in hand, but must be understood differently. One will not go without the other. The Somali state, which includes almost all Somali clans, must be able to build structures capable of supporting a solid and stable state and on the other hand, it is of utmost importance that the FSS encourages and reinforces the Somali nation, undermined by decades of divisions.

To reach these two objectives, we need to find an ethno-political[126] project which, on the one hand, grants the largest autonomy to the regions and on the other hand, for the first time in the known history of the Somalis, initiates a common, customary-based ethnic central power. This idea will be developed below. However it is important to stress now that the critical moment that the Somali nation is undergoing requires a historical restart and a new thinking, as Ali Jimale has highlighted in the preamble of this article. The establishment of this custom based ethnic central power can be the only real evidence that Somalis have accepted to form a real united and reconciled nation: *haan hoostaa laga toola*!

The ethno-political project proposed here has four components: 1) The establishment of a Somali Union Project through the Empowerment of Regions (SUPER), 2) The prioritization of the Conflict Resolution Capacity, 3) The resolution of the Somaliland case; 4) A fundamental change in the Somali clan system.

A Project Based on Traditional Somalis Ecology

The new project has already been unfolding before us since 1991, although it has encountered important opposition, especially from the elite intellectuals and old style politicians[127] and had great difficulty in being implemented. Strangely, foreign scholars have been more accurate and consistent in seeing what has been going on and suggest different options mapping out the future of Somalia. The first study on the topic was published in 1995 by prominent scholars, among them the well-known British anthropologist, Ioan M. Lewis[128], under the title "A study of decentralized political structures for Somalia". Beyond its social and anthropological interest, it is a very informative report for the amount of comparative data it contains and the different options of government it portrays. The real contribution of this work is his intuition, based on his long experience of the Somali context, of the direction of the historical trend of Somali political rebuilding. Lewis says: "The awesome challenge now facing Somalis who seek a wider political structure is to find a way to develop a loose, over-arching framework, capable of providing these minimal common service requirements and at the same time securely rooted in local democratic processes. Clans are the most natural building blocks, here."

In 1999, an article titled "New Hope for Somalia? The Building Block Approach,[129]"mapped out, with striking precision, the present situation with six semi-autonomous territories. The concept of "building blocks" is derived from Lewis & al. (1995). In 1999, there were only three regional states, Somaliland which had declared its independence from Somalia but was not yet recognized as such (and still isn't), Puntland and South-West regional state of Somalia which labeled themselves as regional states. Four years later, Michael van Notten (2003:147) describes how Bosaaso has changed, despite the collapse of the central state of Somalia: "Today, not only are the Somali people more peaceful, but also they are becoming more prosperous than ever before. Bosaaso is a case in point".

And last, let's quote Marleen Renders (2007), whose article "the Appropriate 'governance-technology'?: Somali clan elders and institutions in the making of the 'Republic of Somaliland'", explains how traditional laws and institutions have built a "legitimate, accountable and efficient" state and governance.

Some can be sincerely dubious or skeptical about building the nation on the most divisive of systems (Bulhan, 2008), meaning clanship. But, first, this process is no longer questionable, it is already engaged and has achieved strong results in terms of establishing administrative institutions, "maintenance of law and order, promulgation of constitutional laws and collection of taxes and other public imposts, etc." (Lewis, 1995). Second, it is only the establishment of the first political stratum of the global organization of Somali nation which is discussed here. This political stratum is based on the regions or in other words on kinship, because it is consistent with the traditional and secular policy of Somalis which has brought peace back to Somali territories. Politics is to reconcile reality with an ideal and not just thinking about the latter.

Indeed, "it's arguable whether this traditional system is compatible with the modern political systems, such as multi-party democracy, since kinship based identity politics provide fertile ground for patronage, corruption, nepotism and clannism".[130] However, everybody has now understood "the value of bottom-up approach not only with regard to cost efficiency but also regarding sustainability of solution" (Bulhan, 2013).

Table 6: Dilemma of Somali political governance wavering between centralism and clannism (decentralization)

	Importance of the factor (high=+/ low=-)	
	Period 1	Period 2
Centralism	+	-
Clannism	-	+
Result (Governance)	-	-

Somali Union Project by Empowering Regions (SUPER)

The Somali state policy since 1960 has been characterized by a see-saw effect between state centralism and Clannism[131]. We pointed out the impossibility of ignoring the organizational structure of the society when founding a strong central Somali State. Upon making such a declaration, it is appropriate to solve an equation that summarizes the problem of Somali state governance. It is the real or imaginary relationship between centralism and Clannism. It is often believed that the more the state is centralized, the less important is Clannism and conversely, the less the state is centralized and the more important is Clannism and division among the population. This was summed up in the famous aphorism: *Qaran iyo qabyaalad isma qaadi karaan,* "Nation and clannism are not compatible".

This means that the management or conciliation of the two parameters is part and parcel of the problem. The governance of these seemingly paradoxical parameters will weaken every government, since it is difficult to find the exact balance between Centralism and Clannism. It is important to remember that the successive governments of Somalia since 1960 up to now oscillated between these two parameters, switching from one to the other according to the outcome of the previous government.

Any Somali government, whatever its time and territory, is confronted with these two parameters that seem to oppose Centralism (Ce) and Clannism (Cl): centralism which is justified by the need of unification, and clannism/regionalism which mirrors the local and traditional Somali reality. Each Somali government will increase or decrease the dose of centralism or Clannism according to its political purpose. This situation can be synthesized in a simple equation: Governance = - (Ce x Cl).

Since centralism and clannism are opposite, this equation will always be negative. To get out of this dilemma, Clannism should not be looked at through the restrictive lens of the old ethnocentrism of the West, but should be considered in its sociological, historical and geographical reality. Indeed, Clannism often leads, quite naturally to tribalism and to *familialism*[132] or to an even more restricted system of power sharing, and is in opposition to the republican mode of organization, in its etymological sense. It encourages almost automatically corruption and lack of justice between citizens and it is understandable to see it as a Pandora's Box.

However, all these flaws are integral to every Somali region or Somali territory and it is under the responsibility of every region or territory to put in place the necessary tools and rules to mitigate these hazards associated with Clannism. Again, Clannism has in fact been the only stabilizing anchor of Somali regions after the collapse of the Somali state and it is still functional.

In any case, the relationship between the Central State and the Regional States should be the most federal. Regarding the regional states, the most difficult has been done, since almost all the regions have been created through a bottom-up decision system. The creation phase of these regions, linked by centuries-old systems of traditional solidarity, is a decisive phase, an achievement on which the Somali nation should be constituted. They will either offer the opportunity to boast Somali creativity, innovation and solidarity by founding their policy not on short-term and regional antagonism and competition, but, on a wider national integration process or, they will be the gateway for foreign competition and external interests and the beginning of Somali political disintegration.

The most important and essential step to maintain Somali regional unity, is to put in place a relevant and faithful Conflict Resolution Capacity.

Conflict Resolution Capacity: Modern-Traditional-Islamic

The CRC is not only an essential factor for the reconstruction of Somalia, it is also central for the pacification and unification of the Somali nation. Whether, within a region/territory or between the central state and the regions, there should be a body with this CRC. The exact level of trust put into its composition and its process determines its soundness, the effectiveness of its decisions and its overall efficiency.

This body is not necessarily reducible to the judiciary system (among which are the high court of justice, the constitutional court etc.) but can be also a permanent or an ad hoc body which assists the state(s) to deliberate on serious cases. The system of the council of elders (*Guurti*) or peace-keepers (*Nabad-doon*), offers relevant and efficient bodies which have had positive impacts in some Somali regions. A trans-regional system of this kind can be very helpful in progressing towards rebuilding the State of Somalia.

The only institution which has a political CRC in the FSS is the parliament. But the present process of election of this body, its political purpose and activities and its numbers, are not compatible with peaceful deliberation on complex and strategic issues. It is a fact that, up until today, even the formal structure of the CRC body, namely the Judiciary system, is the major weakness of the FSS institutions. In comparison with the efforts made to establish the Executive System and the Parliament, it is relegated to the background.

The CRC, based on traditional law, with its methodology and its rules (whatever the regional variations), are recognized and accepted by all Somalis, as are also those entrusted with ensuring justice, the legitimate keepers of law such as the Xeer begti (traditional elders).

Sharia-based CRC was applied by Islamic Courts (I.C) during their brief control of Moqadisho in 2006. The town was divided between different warlords and armed militia after the collapse of the central state and within six months, the I.C. achieved outstanding results in pacifying the town and its surroundings. It is said that they "did more to restore order and social progress there than the US has done in Iraq in four years"[133], even if, after "their Medieval-style Islamic version of Sharia law[134]" had infuriated Moqadisho's inhabitants. Generally, though, the Islamic law is normally only used for matrimonial matters (marriage, divorce, family relations, personal material responsibilities and inheritance).

These three legal systems (Modern, Islamic and Traditional) coexist in all Somali territories and regions and operate at different jurisdictional levels. It must be acknowledged that the traditional CRC has remained strong and sometimes inspires greater confidence than the modern CRC in the situation of state fragility. However, it is with the CRC based on the modern law, whether it is inspired by Sharia, traditional Xeer, International laws or not, that the republican state structure, guaranteeing the equality of all before the law, can be reached and established.

The establishment of a robust CRC system should be the top priority of the State of Somalia before the upcoming presidential elections. Regarding conflicts, prevention is, indeed, better than cure and the existence of a credible and effective CRC system is a guarantee of the stability of the institutions which are subjected to the centripetal effect of the power sharing between the regional powers and the Central State. The CRC being a factor of governance, its strength increases or decreases according to that of the government and consequently impacts the SUPER:

Table 7: improving governance through SUPER and CRC[135]

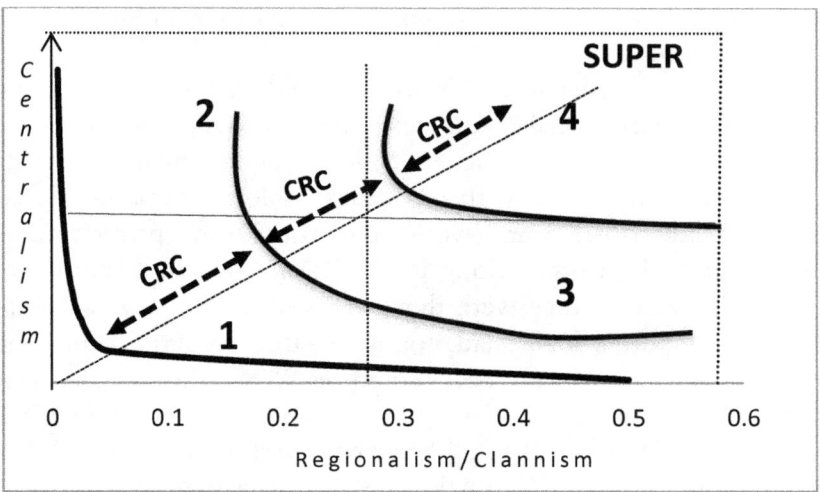

Resolution of the Somaliland Case

The non-resolution of the Somaliland issue has six negative effects:
1) It weakens the Federal State Constitution and leaves it at a draft stage.
2) It weakens also the FSS in view of the regional states and beyond, because it is unable to exercise its sovereignty in all of its territory.
3) It allows foreign countries to take advantage of the rampant but artificial antagonism between Moqadisho and Hargeisa.
4) It entertains the wounds of the civil war and indicates that Somalis have not been able to open a new page.
5) It weakens the development of Somali territory (namely Somaliland) and pushes it to all kinds of adventurous agreements with foreign countries.
6) It delays the reunification of the Somali nation.
These effects are serious and dangerous for the entire Somali nation, because the control of the Horn of Africa is much coveted,[136] as it has always been. It is time to offer a new perspective for the Horn of Africa and for the Somali nation. For all these reasons it is important to get out from the status quo. Until now, the way the discussions between the two parties have been tackled seems to be a dialogue of the deaf, a yes or no deal, a question of take it or leave it, a kind of "Je t'aime, moi non

plus[137]" play. Each party is considering the other party with mistrust or at least as an opponent, instead of seeing it as a partner within its own geostrategic interest.

Somaliland seems eager to obtain its independence in order to have easy access to international loans and aid, to build its necessary infrastructures and cope with the endemic drought which affects its territory. But, it is trite to say that decades of loans have not lifted African and many other third world countries from poverty. The economist Ezenwe Uka was writing in 1993 that "overall Africans are almost as poor today as they were thirty years ago.[138]" Many scholars have shown that public loans had not necessarily favoured economic growth in Sub-Saharan African (SSA) countries. While the external debt stock of these countries has regularly grown from US$67 billion in 1980, to reach US$360 billion in 2013[139], "the growth performance of SSA has been deteriorating with GDP growth rates kept at a minimum or even below zero in some cases.[140]" This means that there is no systematic co-relation between loans and development. In contrast, the direct relation between good governance and development has been thoroughly established[141].

Second, Somaliland has experimented with an original process of indigenous state building, with efficient economic growth based on no loan and no interest policy. So far, this growth is not sufficient to create enough jobs for the youth and enhance the poor living standards of its population, but its political innovation and its democratic experiences are sound foundations for building a relevant economic and social system, with the appropriate institutions of control and public policy assessment before loading young generations with unbearable loans. In other words, it is most essential to ensure strongly engrained good governance before contracting international loans. That is the natural process to achieve equitable development.

Third, if Somaliland dreams of just steaming off from the rest of the Somali territories and severing historical relationships, it is a naïve and extremely hazardous strategy. In fact, Ethiopia is growing economically and logically, according to the Core-Periphery Theory, it expands into territorial holdings of the neighbours which it has. The recent tripartite agreement over the port of Berbera is an obvious proof of the validity of Ethiopia as a core nation. A core nation is a hegemonic nation which "is able to impose its set of rules on the interstate system and thereby create a world political order as it thinks wise."[142] Ethiopia and Kenya, backed or not by their foreign allies, are trying their best to reinforce their positions as core nations in the Horn of Africa.

Somaliland as well as Djibouti, amidst the intense geostrategic game of the Horn of Africa, will either turn to become clients of Ethiopia or try to counterbalance the strong growing influence of this country with another core position. In any case, Somaliland has only two alternatives, either become a client of Ethiopia or to renew the contract with Moqadisho not only to build back their lost core position, but to strengthen it considerably.

The only way to achieve that is to move from the second stage of John Friedmann's Stages of growth[143] to the third stage:

Figure 3: John Friedmann's Stages of growth

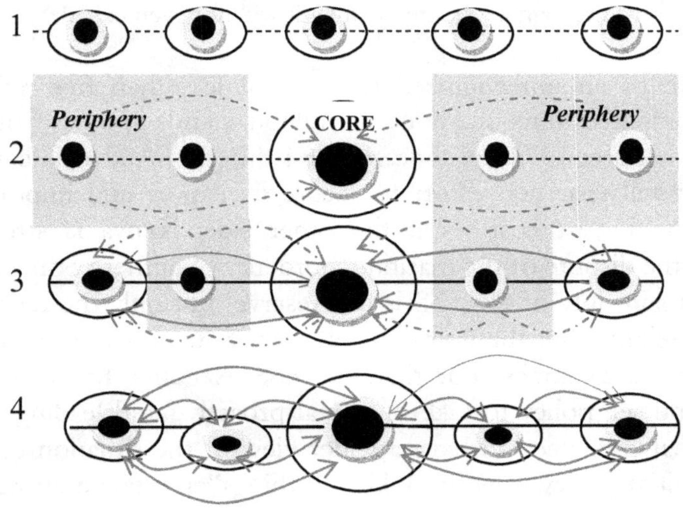

Source: Friedmann's (1966) Core-Periphery Model.

The third stage corresponds to the creation of regional sub-centers which will reinforce the core position of the Somali territory.. Before trying to discuss how to achieve that goal, it is important to highlight the FSS's part in the solution of Somaliland issue.

In 1992, Somaliland withdrew officially from the SUPP. Twenty years later, the Federal State of Somalia, in 2012, erased the SUPP project from its provisional constitution and abandoned it. In 2017, when the

FSS handed over Abdikarim Sheikh Muse, "Qalbi Dhagax", to the Federal State of Ethiopia, it was the obvious sign that the SUPP had truly come to an end.

Ethiopia is "planning to build several large dams for hydropower generation and large scale irrigation schemes[144]" on Juba and Shabelle Rivers and this will put significant stress on water supply in Southern Somalia. In 1963, the Ethiopian prime minister declared at the Organization of African Unity in Addis-Ababa:

> The historical frontiers of Ethiopia stretched from the Red Sea to the Indian Ocean, including all the territory between them. That is a fact. There is no record in history either of a Somali State or a Somali nation. I regret to say it, but that too is a fact. An international treaty regulates the frontiers between the two countries. If the Somali Republic does not recognize the treaty, then it will not even exist.[145]

That a portion of an unrecognized territory of less than five million inhabitants, compared to its one hundred million, stands in its way of the sea is indeed a source of deep concern for Ethiopia. And it is certain that the latter will spare no effort to secure its export and import of products at the lowest cost. On the other side, Kenya is strongly committed to the dispute of the maritime borders of Southern Somalia.[146]

First, the main duty of the FSS is to preserve, not only the territory under its sovereignty, but the unity of the entire Somali nation which is going through critical times. For that, the FSS executive has to move from a wait-and-see policy to take on a real proactive and leading role. That means that they need to have a wider view of the situation of the Somalis, to "initiate a new way of looking at things" and come up with a real political project.

Considering this situation, the FSS should seriously consider the self-determination of the Somaliland territory, because this territory has already been, for almost three decades, functioning as an independent state. Meles Zenawi saved Ethiopia from disintegration because he had taken a decisive political initiative by proposing "self-determination" to every indigenous nation who claims it through a regular process. Politics is not a matter of management, but a matter of clairvoyance, proactive ideas and courage.

Finding a solution for the issue of Somaliland will mean for the FSS to take over leadership of the destiny of the Somali nation and open a new era. If it chooses the status quo as a solution, it means that it leaves the destiny of Somali territories in the hands of the African core nations (Ethiopia and Kenya) and those of the Gulf States.

If Somaliland has no other strategy than to avoid union with the FSS and FSS has no other vision than the old SUPP which is already dead, this is a bad game for all of the Somali nation. Instead, they both need to work on how to constitute a core or double-core nation, by satisfying each party's essential target. If there is not a strong enough agreement for mutual solidarity and a significant move on from the status quo, the Somali nation will again lose another historical opportunity to control its destiny[147] and to live under the governance of its most valuable rule and institution which could be identified as those of the liberty and poetry.

The second part of the revitalization of the Somali union project should be based on its customary laws and traditional institutions. Without this second part, the SUPER, the aims of which are the pacification and unification of the Somali nation, will remain an empty rhetorical exercise. The real revitalization of this nation needs a fundamental change.

The Fundamental Change: Constituting the Supra-Clan Segment

From what has been said so far, there are at least two obvious facts which made this change necessary: 1) Somali ethnic organization framework has not changed significantly for centuries, although its environment has undergone tremendous change, the core constitution of the major Somali clans is still the same and have still the same type of inter-clannic relations;
2) Somalis have not been able to transform their ethnic unity (linguistic, cultural and religious) into a common central State.

In this essay, we have highlighted that the modern Somali state was submitted into two antagonistic forces   a clan centrifugal force and a state centripetal one. And the relation between these two forces has been (from the 60s until now) similar to that of a pendulum or the regular turning of an hourglass. In 1992, the centrifugal force was the strongest and drew the new map of the present Somali state. But naturally the Somali state is committed to re-inverse the momentum of this hourglass move, to reach a balance between clan power and central state power, recalling the Sisyphus' myth.[148] Indeed, if Sisyphus should not change his mind and come to a fundamental change, he will suffer eternally.

This fundamental change will come from one observation only that Somalis are divided from the bottom. Somaliness has no formal foundation. This is why Somalis lack the stratum segment of their ontological ethnos and this is why they have never been able to establish one shared state. The clans are the real constitutional segments of the Somali nation and there is no social contract between these clans. There have been various "social contracts" between political leaders belonging to different clans, but they did not have the customary legitimacy to speak on the behalf of their clan. These politicians have usurped the traditional leaders by disqualifying them as being regressive and preventing them from applying the SUPP.

Thus Somali society, being divided at the root by different clans, has never succeeded in establishing a central state. However, there is one Somali clan which underwent an important change in its political and ecological environment, several centuries ago and came up with the most original and most efficient social innovation, the establishment of a supra segmental law, the Xeer Issa. The Somali nation is now going through a historical phase which needs such a fundamental adaptive change if it is to survive as such.

Somali-Issa Clan Constitution Model

Somali-Issa[149] clannic organization can serve as a model for this fundamental change, for six reasons, at least:
1) The Issa have an oral corpus of law, the Xeer Ciise, which covers every aspect of life[150] and is remarkable because of : " la rigueur de sa structuration et la codification de ses lois, mais aussi par le rôle qu'il joue dans les fondements de la 'Démocratie pastoral' des Issas"[151] (A. M. Iye, 417);
2) It is one of the rare Somali clan whose Ugaas, or King, is not chosen through succession but by selection, according to a rigorous and strict procedure; 3) It is the only Somali family-clan that has one single Ugaas, recognized by all members of the community;
4) The Somali-Issa have not been protagonists in the Somali civil war and have no unresolved historical dispute with another Somali clan;
5) The corpus of the Xeer draws its content from the high tradition and wisdom of the Somalis; although old, it is extremely modern;

6) The circumstances of the appearance of this Xeer strangely resemble those that prevail today in Somali territories. A. M. Iye explains that it was formalized in the 16th century which corresponds to :« un tournant important dans l'Histoire de la Corne de l'Afrique [avec] des bouleversements capitaux au niveau ethnique, culturel, social et économique, sans parler des transformations politiques : faillites de la conquête d'Abyssinie [sic], déroute des armées musulmanes, déferlements des Gallas dans le Nord de la Corne et éclatement d'épidémies meurtrières… .»[152]

These similarities between the two periods are not the only ones, as we can read in Iye's article:

> « Le Xeer Issa est née en cette période de troubles et de décadence, qui s'est traduite par la montée de l'insécurité dans les villes et l'effritement des codes et de la législation qui régissaient les Etats musulmans de la côte….Les centres urbains furent désertés au profit des campagnes devenues plus sûres. Ce qui conduisit à une retribalisation des populations citadines. C'est à la suite de ces bouleversements que certains tribus somalis cités par les chroniqueurs disparurent et que d'autres jusqu'à là inconnues émergèrent… Le Xeer Issa est le produit de cette retribalisation. »[153]

Within the corpus of the Xeer have been mentioned the four reasons why the Issa had decided to come together and establish this Xeer. It is said that it was because four scourges had increased considerably: damac, duulimaad, *dil iyo dhac*,[154] meaning "envy, attacks, killing and plunder." There is a logical relation between these four types of scourges, first comes envy, then the attack, followed by the killing and finally the plunder and robbery.

Today, we could find ourselves almost in the same situation. The Horn of Africa is subjected to an intense competition between regional and international countries, Southern Somalia and especially Somalia's capital is constantly under attack from extremists controlled by foreign forces and the natural resources of Somalia are the targets of obvious covetousness and competition.

Initially, the Issa do not all hail from the same genealogical filiations concerning the six large sub-clans. Only half are considered to go back to the same eponymous forefather, Sheikh Issa. These are the Three Issa or 'Saddexda Ciise'. They are called Ceeleye, Hawla Qaade and Holle. The other three tribal groups, the Wardiq, Horoone, and Uurweyne, joined the confederation. By this unifying act, one of the most important Somali clans was founded.

Ibraahim Axmad Cali (2016: 114)[155] reports that the first man, who put forward the proposal to undertake the search for a King for the whole clan, was inspired by three insect species which have a Chief, *Horjooge* and have an astonishing social organization, namely the bees, the ants and the termites. From then on, the Issa, inspired by the efficient social organization of these natural species, got their King. But before choosing their King, they first established the Xeer. To finalize this customary law, it took long years of palaver in different places and required a lot of sacrifices to support such long meetings. Resuming Ali M. Iye (1988, 1990) and Cabdalla Xaaji (2010), Sagal M. Djama (2014)[156] and Ibraahim Axmad Cali (2016), we will highlight some of the founding principles of the Xeer Issa and its possible adaptation to the entire Somali nation.

A few Founding Principles of Somali-Issa Xeer

Equality before the law

This principle is clearly established by the saying: *Ciise waa Ciise, cidna cid caaro ma dheera,* "An Issa is an Issa, no one is superior to another". To paraphrase it and extend it to all members of the Somali nation, we can say *"Soomaali waa soomaali, cidna cid caaro ma dheera".* This is the first founding principal.

Another assertion establishes the equality of all Issa sub-clans: *Ciise marti ma ahee, magan ma laha,* "Issa knows about hospitality, but has no refugee". This means that no one needs to be under the protection of any other clan, all the clans are equal, regardless to their numeral importance. The sub-clans have the same number of representatives in the two institutions of the Xeer, the Guddi (Council of the Elders) and the Gande (Council of the Sages)[157], except the Eleye sub-clan, considered as the elder of Issa clan and the Wardiiq sub-clan, from which the Ugaas is chosen. From each of these last two sub-clans, come seven members of the councils, whereas all the four other sub-clans have six members each.[158]

The members of the Gande, which is the supreme council, no longer belong to their respective sub-clans, since the "blood price" has been paid to their kinship[159]. They have been selected in accordance to certain moral principles and their decisions are expected to be impartial and conform to the Xeer.

The Importance of the Law

There are many sayings that underline in one way or the other, the role and importance of law among the Somali-Issa: *Eebbehay xogun buu iga abuuray, Aabbahayna xeer buu ii dhigay which means*, "God made me from a seed, and my father gave me the Xeer". The Xeer is thus the creative act of human beings, a noble heritage from the ancestors. Outside the law, Man is just an animal, as another adage of the corpus emphasizes: *Xeer la'aan waa la xooloobaa*, "being without law makes you become a livestock". And no one is above the law, not even the King: *Xeer waa kaa sarreeyaaye lagama sarreeyo*, "the law is superior to you, but no one is superior to the law ". This emphasizes again on the notion of everyone's equality in front of the law, whatever the social position of the person may be.

Principle of Commonality[160]

This principle is in fact the core foundation of the unity of the Community. It establishes three things that the Issa have in common: *Ciise saddex baa u dhax 'ah: dhulka, martida iyo Ugaaska*, "The Issa share three things: "land, hospitality and the Ugaas." Land belongs to God and no one has the right to take it for his own. The hospitality is a social obligation which is fixed according to certain rules and the Ugaas belongs to the whole community.

Selection and role of the Ugaas[161]

After the establishment of the first version of the Xeer, then came the decision of "catching" the King. The Issa did not speak about "electing" or "choosing" but about "catching" the King. Because the King's position is not seen as a sinecure, as it has usually been seen in modern days, but almost as a "priesthood" based functionality and no reasonable and sincere man will easily accept to take on such a burden. The Ugaas could be, in fact a Philosopher-King, according Plato's conception which was developed in the Republic, who could accept this burden only for the sake of his nation. As Iye puts it rightly, the Ugaas "has more obligations towards his subjects than privileges from them."[162]

The main characteristic of the King is to "preside and not to decide": *Ugaasku wuu guddoomiyaa ee ma gooyo*. The decision belongs to the assembly, which is not divided into opposing parties, but observes the general interest of the community based on "consensus". As for the Ugaas, the mag, "blood price" is paid to his kinsmen, which means that the King does no longer belong to them, just as a dead person does not any longer belong to his/her relatives. He belongs henceforth to the whole clan and is only subject to the Xeer.

The Ugaas is, first and foremost, a JUST man, someone who guides his people according to the Xeer, to the right path. This is why he is first of all a man inspired by the fear of God and whose blessings and prayers are an important part of his office. The Xeer establishes the procedure for "capturing" the King", and defines some physical and moral characteristics which are the pre-requiste for every future King.

The procedure to "catch the Ugaas" is an original and complex one which is described here by Iye:

> "The Ugaas is chosen from a given clan by a special assembly of wise men after a long and laborious selection where the "sciences" such as astrology, divination, cabalistics and the interpretation of dreams are solicited in order to identify "the chosen one" corresponding to defined objective and metaphysical criteria. It is a procedure similar to the one for choosing the Tibetan Dalai Lama. To make the function of the king even less attractive, the Xeer provides, for example, the ritual of the abduction of the future king. It is a surprise assault on the camp of the future king, which takes place at dawn and consists of taking away from his family and against his will; the Ogaas is often chosen quite young."[163]

The mode of "catching" the King and the rules attached to his powers specified by the Xeer neutralize the abuse of such power which normally results from long lasting power.

Some Principles about Foreign Policy

We have pointed out the historical context in which the Xeer appears, and specially the strong pressure that the Somali Issa community experienced as a result of the defeat of the Muslim kingdoms in the 16th century and the great movement of the Oromo community to the west of the Somalis. The few adages below show that the founding fathers of the Xeer Issa were not some illiterate camel herders unaware of international relations and diplomatic affairs. Instead, they seem to have had sound and subtle knowledge of these issues on which they base their interaction with foreigners:
- *Nin hantidaada doonayaa hubkaaga looma dhiibto*, "Someone who wants to take up your property, you do not entrust your weapons"
- *Nin bakhtigaaga doonayaa, baahidaada looma sheegto*, "One should not tell one's needs to someone who wishes one's death"
- *Nin dalkaaga doonaya, dawyadaada lama baro*," To someone who want to conquer your country, you do not show your ways"

The kind of attitude expressed in these adages, appearing as a sense of mistrust towards westerners, during colonization, may have made them appear primitive and savage[164]. But in fact, this attitude may have helped them keep their distance from the influence of all foreigners, namely the Ethiopia different regimes, the Arabs and the Westerners who impacted more thoroughly on the coastal regions of the Somali territories.

It is unfortunate that the Issa monarchy has not been well studied until recently and especially how this monarchy faced colonialism. For instance, in a comparative perspective, the 17th Ugaas of the Issa, Ugaas Wahays, reigned during the exact same period that Sayid Mohamed Abdalla Hassan led his public activates in the Dervish movement. These two leaders had different strategies and different backgrounds but were motivated by the same opposition against the unjust domination of the colonial powers. Both of them were rejected by their communities and killed during their struggle against their colonialist opponents. In fact, Ugaas Wahays personally refused to pay tithes to the Ethiopian monarchy, after the Guddi accepted to pay them. The Ugaas was then jailed, with his immediate followers, and died in jail a short time later[165]. Five years after the end of the tragic end of Ugaas Wahays, Ugaas Hassan Hirsi was enthroned. He reigned from 1928 to 1994.

It is undoubtedly the factor of the longevity which makes the difference between the Dervish, in power for a limited period of time and the Issa Monarchy which, by its duration, will allow this clan to cross the very troubled period of the 20th century and occupy the place it has today in the clan configuration of the Somalis.

Thanks to this monarchy, the Issa community, especially in rural areas, has safeguarded not only the ancient Xeer, but also the usage of authentic Somali names, and some of the ancient Somali cultural traits, such as the usage of a solar calendar, astrology and divinatory practices for important events, such as the selection of the Ugaas[166].

Sealing Reconciliation

A. M. Iye explains that formal reconciliation after the Xeer verdict and the payment of compensation is not sufficient. According to the spirit of the Xeer, what should be reached through the verdict is to "heal the wound"[167] from the hearts. For that, Iye says that it is important that "each have the feeling for having gained something".

We may rather easily understand how the victim can win something since he/she will get compensation after the verdict, but how can the guilty person win something and what is the purpose of this principle ? First, even the guilty person has the right to solidarity from his/her kinsmen. Second, the alleged offender has to be convinced of his/her guilt. Since truth and justice are more important than filiation, as a Somali-Issa adage says, "testify against your brother but then pay with him the penalty", the guilty person will gain the solidarity of his/her kinsmen, if he/she is convicted of the crime he/she is accused of. Third, there is a whole ceremony preparing the deliberations which aim to safeguard the solidarity and the cohesion of the community. This gives, even to the guilty person, the feeling of belonging to the whole community.

The traditional law of the Somali-Issa, even if it needs to be updated to take into account the trans-clan and the modern and urban way of life of the Somalis, contains the principles and regulations which can serve as a social contract between all Somalis. Among these provisions, the most notable being those which concern the mode of election of the King, the governance of the pastoral monarchy and the relations with foreign parties. It is a legacy of the greatest value which can help the Somali nation to overcome these hard times it is currently going through. The elders have left this jewel, the Xeer, which is applicable to the whole community, wherever it lives and under whatever political power it could be subjected to.

6. General Conclusion

Implementing the SUPER: The Natural Path for Somali State Building

We have shown that the SUPP was based on a vision which promotes a centralized state, thwarting the centrifugal effect of clan exercise. Since 2000, the Central Somali State has been rebuilding on more "decentralized" principles. The pacification and the establishment of public institutions, based on these principles, in the Somali regions show that this approach is more efficient than the one experienced during the former regimes.

A hard and dangerous stage has been passed through, as the different regions have been created. The important next step is to review the Provisional Constitution according to a bottom-up decision. This constitution should not be or be seen as a document "crafted outside Somalia, under the sponsorship and patronage of foreign countries, including some with longstanding strategic and geopolitical ambitions in the country."[168] It needs to be deeply engrained in the Somali indigenous political organisation and in the social, cultural and economic reality of this nation, to make it workable.

The issue of Somaliland needs to be tackled and resolved. As long as there is an unresolved dispute between Somaliland and the FSS, this grain of division and discord will still be alive among Somalis. Foreign countries with geostrategic ambitions regarding the Horn of Africa will take advantage of this division. It is well known that colonialism thrives on the divisions and antagonisms between the members of the communities it wants to dominate.

A complete lap of the SUPP has been done and the Somali nation has come back almost at the same situation as in the colonization period. So, it is time to set the record straight and take the proper direction. In this essay, we have assumed that this direction can be based on a twofold project, one which is on the political level, which has been presented as being the SUPER and the other which is on the ethnic level, which is the constitution of the missing segment of the Somali clan system, the supra clannic segment.

Constituting the Supra-Clannic Segment (CSCS)

The great paradox of the Somali nation, always observed by many analysts, is that although being a very homogeneous nation, it is one the most divided nations in Africa, making it difficult to govern. This paradox is obvious due to the fact that the Somali nation is divided from the root. There is no formal segment unifying all the Somali clans, in spite of the existence of the unifying and trans-tribal term "Somali". So there is a need for a supra-clannic segment which could be still missing, something that unifies all clans and makes effective the concept of "Soomaalinimo".

The clans which have different histories (real or mystified) have never been unified, although every clan claims to be member of the "Somali nation". The basis of this unification is instead strong, since a tremendous part of Somalis have the same lingua franca, share the same cultural core deriving from Islam and from an agro-pastoral way of life and live in a contiguous space.

The colonization of the Somali nation was possible because, among other reasons, colonizing powers used to deal with clans separately, taking advantage of the antagonisms and competitions between these clans, to reinforce their positions in the occupied territories. And Somali religious, intellectual and political leaders, who thought they were building a unified nation, had not begun from the bottom which had been the basis of the Somali nation, meaning the clan system. It is why even if the Somali history of the last century has been tumultuous and full of hardships, in its most part, there has been no change at the macro-level clan system of the Somalis. Indeed, there have been clan or sub-clan coalitions inside parties or political movements, but the five or six family clans have not changed since time immemorial. Clans and sub-clans seem to continue their competitions in rural areas regarding wells and grazing and in urban areas concerning political power.

The collapse of the State of Somalia resulted in bloody confrontations between clans and sub-clans. However, except through superficial handshakes and emotional discourses, effective reconciliation has not been reached, no structural clan system change has been introduced. Only the political system has been modified, passing from a centralized state to a federal state. But the fundamental basis of Somali division has not been even briefly addressed, not to speak about changing it.

Considering the historical stage of Somali history and the multitude of foreign pressure that this nation is undergoing presently, it is necessary to interrogate its basic foundation. From that point of view, we have seen how the Somali-Issa in 16th century changed its clan based structure by introducing a unifying supra segment which permitted them to cope with the harsh reality of their time.

The constitution of this Supra-Clannic Segment (CSCS), through the composition of the necessary organs and above all the "capture" of a Just man, a King, shared by all Somalis, will end an old chapter of Somali history and open a new one. Traditional leaders have the moral duty to consider seriously the grave situation in which this nation is today and generate new hope for it. This nation is fortunate to have in its midst a community that has the necessary know-how to help or to carry out such an anthropological project.

With such a project, the score indicating the general situation of the Somali nation would be higher than it has ever been during its whole history. It will have at least the score 21, compared to the score 18 of the period 1960-1975, which was the period where Soomaalino was the strongest:

Table 9: Soomaalinimo concept impact through CSCS

	(a) Political Situation of the territory	(b) Ethnic diversity	(c) Somalis/ other ethnic groups	(d) Clan diversity	(e) Soomaalinimo concept impact	(f) SUPER	Score
Djibouti	Recognized State	Relative Heterogeneity	Majority	Relative Homogeneity	Strong	On The Agenda	5
NE-Kenya (NEK)	Decentralized Counties	Heterogeneity	Minority	Heterogeneity	Strong	On The Agenda	3
Somali Region of Ethiopia (SRE)	Decentralized Region	Heterogeneity	Minority	Heterogeneity	Strong	On The Agenda	3
Somaliland	(Un)recognized State[169]	Homogeneity	Majority	Relative Homogeneity	Strong	On The Agenda	5
Somalia	Federal State	Relative Homogeneity	Majority	Heterogeneity	Strong	On The Agenda	5
TOTAL	Somali Nation General Situation						21

Finally, it is necessary to stress that the CSCS respects five principles:

a) It is not meant to lead to the disunity of any other nation and should not be done against any other nation.
b) It does not need to be recognized by others and should be based on indisputable facts.
c) It is in concord with Somalis secular traditional laws
d) It is in concord with international laws

This last principle is not the least, and concerns the CSCS implementation: it should be free from any foreign intervention. It should be funded, organized and fulfilled by the Somali community itself. If the SUPER is not accompanied by this necessary and complementary approach to reshape the Somali national clan based structure (meaning the CSCS), in order to give it a common destiny, this nation will be more divided than it has ever been. The geopolitical interests attracted to the Horn of Africa, and especially the Somali-speaking area which is one of the most strategic shipping lanes for international maritime trade, will create antagonisms more severe than ever. The nation will be divided into territories, regions and clans, competing more forcefully than in the 19th and the 20th century, because they will be backed by different countries, each with its own interests.

If any initiative is not taken, specifically by the Federal State or the Somali traditional leaders, the natural process defined in the Core-Periphery theory will take place. And from this perspective, Somaliland and the South West of Somalia will follow the process of being attracted in the ever expanding influence of Ethiopia, whereas the far South of Somalia will end up as a Kenyan satellite, which can help this latter country make a serious claim on the disputed area around the Somali border[170].

Somali Culture: Advantage or Hindrance to Change

The proposition presented here is based on the vision on culture detailed on the first part of this book. It is stated there that there are three main constituents of culture which are environment, education[171] and experience. These constitutions are common to all living organisms, from the cell to the most developed mammals, and are the necessary equipment for this living organism to survive, first, and then to develop itself until its uppermost stage.

But the living organism is urged by two contradictory forces:

...the living being is continuously moving from one environment to another: i.e. from the mother womb environment, to that of the nuclear family, and to that of a larger social environment, and finally to that of national and more global ecosystems. There is the necessity of life, the "life force" which needs continuously to grow up and go from one environment to an ever larger and more complex one, to satisfy greater individual pleasures or needs. In other words, when a being becomes mature and fully adapted to one environment, it passes to the higher environment. But it is also confronted with the opposite tendency induced by the self-preservation instinct which considers "openness" as a risk for one's life. It is the dilemma in which the individual is confronted with the compulsion towards widening one's space of interaction to have a more exciting life and weighing it against the risk against one's preservation. Going through a new environment and getting adapted to it requires more energy and this presents the risk of the unknown, the dangers to one's self-preservation.[172]

If a culture becomes deficient to deal with these contradictory tendencies and lacks sufficient strength to permit its members to take appropriate decisions to cope with their environment, this culture cannot survive as such. Its members will, in a more or less short time, become "subject to an exogenous cultural domination or a cultural shift." The obvious influence on the Somali traditional Islamic belief by the "rising influence of Saudi Arabia in global politics[173]" is in fact a first sign of the kind of cultural influence which is already in process. The change of Somali modern arts, specially the losing importance of Somali Theater and musical concerts, are some observable facts. It is not a matter of judgment, but a matter of factual observations.

References

[125] From Ramana Maharshi.
[126] In African studies, there is a tendency to ethnicize all areas of knowledge: ethno-medicine, ethno-politics, ethno-philosophy, etc., which sometime reminds old terminology used in the 19th century anthropology. Here we are just talking about two aspects that are

closely related, the ethnic structure and the state structure, but belong to two separate spheres of organization and responsibilities.

[127] See The ITPCM International *Commentary Somalia Clan and State Politics*, Vol. IX no. 34, 2013.

[128] We are aware that some of Lewi's contributions for Somali studies have been under critics by Somali scholars (cf. Ahmed Qasim Ali, 1995). We consider, with Jimale (2010), that Lewis work has not to be "vilified nor canonized" and should be tackled with critical approach like every scientific works.

[129] Bryden Matt, 1999, "New Hope for Somalia?" *Review of African Political Economy*, Vol. 26, No. 79, Africa and the Drugs Trade(Mar., pp. 134-140, Published by: Taylor & Francis, Ltd. http://www.jstor.org/stable/4006529

[130] Adam Haji-Ali Ahmed, "Internal and external challenges to peace for Somaliland" IN *Somalia Clan and State Politics*, 2013, ITPCM International Commentary.

[131] These words can be replaced by *nationalism* and *regionalism*, or by other words expressing the dichotomy stressed here. Clannism is meant here the traditional mode of Somali organization and for the moment we would like to keep this term which is more meaningful for the dichotomy we would like to highlight.

[132] Understood as a political regime which is a more restricted form of nepotism.

[133] Said S Samatar (2007) "The Islamic Courts and Ethiopia's Intervention in Somali: Redemption or Adventurism?", https://www.chathamhouse.org/sites/files/chathamhouse/public/Research/Africa/250407samatar.pdf

[134]*Ibid.*

[135] The four positions which are high-lightened with numbers 1 to 4 represent different types of State governance. They can be interpreted, with some simplifications, as follows: 1-autocratic regime (like the Siyad Barre's regime), 2-parliamentarian (like the first Somalia governments, from 1960-67), 3- Federal governance with strong regional states (present situations), 4- Strong Federal state with well-balanced sharing power between center and regions, with political parties playing much role than clans in the political system.

The dynamic move from one position to another is operated by the growing Conflict Resolution Capacity (CRC), which itself has to move from traditional judiciary to modern judicial system.

[136] https://www.mondialisation.ca/djibouti-declencheur-dune-destabilisation-trans-regionale/5624182

[137] Words from a well-know French song, by Serge Gainsbourg, which means "I love you! Nor do I".

[138] Ezenwe, Uka (1993) : The african debt crisis and the challenge of development, Intereconomics, Nomos Verlagsgesellschaft, Vol. 28, Iss. 1, pp. 35-43, Baden-Baden.

[139] Iinternationnal Monetary Fund (2015) quoted by Sakina Hamid,(2015): The impact of foreign debt on economic growth in Sub-Saharan Africa, Strathmore University.

[140] Mahlet Kassaye (2015), *"The Effect Of External Debt On Economic Growth In Sub-Saharan Africa"*, PhD Thesis, Addis Ababa University.

[141] Al-jurf, S. (2010), "Good governance & transparency: Their impacts on development." Retrieved from http://www.uiowa.edu/ifdebook/ebook2/contents/part2-V.shtml; Lawal, G., & Tobi, A. (2006). Bureaucratic corruption, good governance and development: The challenges and prospects of institution building in Nigeria. Journal of Applied Sciences Research, 2(10), 642-649.

[142] Wallerstein (2011 [1980]: xxii) *The Modern World-System II: Mercantilism and the Consolidation of the European World-Economy, 1600–1750.* Berkeley: University of California Press.

[143] Friedmann John (1966) "Regional development policy : a case study of Venezuela", M.I.T. Press, Cambridge Mass.

[144] A. Elmi Mohamed (2013) "Managing shared river basins in the Horn of Africa: Ethiopian planned water projects on the Juba and Shabelle rivers and effects on downstream uses in Somalia", WIT Transactions on Ecology and The Environment, Vol 172, WIT Press.
https://www.witpress.com/Secure/elibrary/papers/RBM13/RBM13012FU1.pdf

[145] Kendie Daniel (2007), « Towards Resolving the Ethiopia-Somalia Disputes", International Conference on African Development

Archives. Paper 104. http://scholarworks.wmich.edu/africancenter_icad_archive/104.

[146] *Cf.* Report of the International Court of Justice, (Feb, 2, 2017). Maritime Delimitation In The Indian Ocean, (Somalia vs. Kenya)

[147] Hassan A. Keynan (2018) "Can Somali sovereignty and unity be saved? Analysis and recommendations", WardheerNews, 31 Marsh 2018.

[148] Sisyphus was condemned to push a rock up a mountain, which always ended up descending the slope again, leading Sisyphus to resume his task indefinitely.

[149] The name of this clan is written differently according to scholars and the language used (Somali, French or English). In the article we will use these different transcriptions: Ciise, Issa, Isse.

[150] *Cf.* Ali Moussa Iye who says that this Xeer « is made up of a Criminal Code, a political Constitution and of a Code of conduct, to restore peace and ensure the practice of a democratic power », translated from: https://www.alimoussaiye.com/blog-ecrits--publications/le-xeer-quels-enseignements-pour-la-construction-dune-gouvernance-dmocratique-endogne

[151] C. M. Iye (1988), « Le Xeer Issa : Etude d'un contrat pastoral traditionnel », *In Proceedings of the Third International Congress of Somali Studies*, Ed. Annarita Puglielli, Roma : Pensiero Scientifico Editore. The quote can be translated as: "the rigor of its structuring and the codification of its laws, but also by the role it plays in the foundations of the "pastoral democracy... "

[152] "...important turning point in the history of the Horn of Africa [with] the total upheavals at the ethnic, cultural, social and economic level, not to mention the political transformations: failure of the conquest of Abyssinia [sic], defeat of the Muslim armies, the massive arrival of the Gallas in the Northern Horn and outbreak of deadly epidemics ... "

[153] *Ibid.* "The Xeer Issa was born in this period of turmoil and decadence, which resulted in rising insecurity in the cities and the erosion of codes and legislation that ruled the Muslim states of the coast .... The urban centers were deserted in favor of the safer countryside. This led to a retribalization of urban populations. It was as a result of these upheavals that some Somali tribes quoted by the chroniclers

disappeared and that others until then (unknown) emerged ... The Xeer Issa is the product of this retribalization."

[154] Cabdallah Xaaji Cusmaan (2010), Djibouti, p:5.

[155] Ibraahim Axmad Cali(2016), *Aaya-reeb : Kab dhexeeye, Sooyaalka Xeer Ciise,* ISBN 9791092933048, Djibouti.

[156] Sagal Hassan Djama (2014), *Eléments d'éthnographie d'un people somali de la Corne de l'Afrique: autour des cérémonies d'intronisation du XIXe Ugaas des 'Isē* (Ethiopie, Djibouti, Somaliland), PhD, Université de Metz, France.

[157] These two councils have different roles and different procedures.

[158] It seems, as we understand from Sagal Hassan Djama thesis (2014:193-195), that the supplementary members granted to Eleye and Wardiiq sub-clans, is more justified by the desire to reach the symbolic figure of forty-four. Besides, the number of the *Guddi*, "the council of the Elders", can vary but the same proportion will be observed to reach specific number of members.

[159] This payment can be symbolic and not effective.

[160] Ali M. Iye (2013), « Le Xeer : quels enseignements pour la construction d'une gouvernance démocratique endogène ? » https://www.alimoussaiye.com/blog-ecrits--publications/le-xeer-quels-enseignements-pour-la-construction-dune-gouvernance-dmocratique-endogne

[161] *See* the excellent thesis on the subject conducted by Sagal Mohamed Djama (2014).

[162] A. M. Iye, 2013, *ibid.* Author translation (AT).

[163] A. M. Iye, 2013, *ibid.* Author translation.

[164] Kadar Ali Diraneh, 2016, *Regards Croisés Entre Colonisateurs Et Colonisés : Français et Djiboutiens dans la littérature,* L'Harmattan, Paris ; Moussa Souleiman Obsieh, 2012, *L'oralité dans la littérature de la Corne de l'Afrique : traditions orales, formes et mythologies de la littérature pastorale, marques de l'oralité dans la littérature,* Thesis, PhD : https://tel.archives-ouvertes.fr/tel-00796155/document

[165] Sagal Mohamed Djama, 2014:234-237, *Ibid.*

[166] Ibraahim Axmad Cali (2018), *Aaya-reeb II : Cirmaalka Buraad,* ISBN 97992933147, Djibouti.

[167] A. M. Iye (2013), *ibid*. The translation is from the author of the present book.

[168] Hassan A. Keynan (2018), "Can Somali sovereignty and unity be saved? Analysis and recommendations", WardheerNews. http://www.wardheernews.com/can-somali-sovereignty-and-unity-be-saved-analysis-and-recommendations/

[169] The status of this territory will depend on the conflict resolution capacity (CRC) of the two parties. The spirit of this twofold project is also to find a solution on this case too.

[170] See the interesting article of Hassan A. Keynan (*op. cit.*) who gives some possible evolutions " if the status quo remains the same" and radical decisions are not taken.

[171] Processus of Learning.

[172] In Chapter I- *New insights on culture* (in this book).

[173] Abdurahman M. Abdullahi (Baadiyow), (2015), *The Islamic movement in Somalia: a study of the Islah Movement, 1950-2000*, Adonis & Abbey Publishers, London.

BOOK REVIEW

Dr. Ali Jimale Ahmed

Catastrophic events force/compel survivors to rethink the contours and shapes of their lives. They understand that without a rigorous and methodical re-examining of the calamity and its impact on their psychosomatic being, they would not be able to structure a viable way out. The learned among the survivors, as the vanguard of society, come to realize the need to go back to the drawing board and re-examine the residual remains of a tradition in the midst of anomie. They attempt to derive meaning from the charred remains of collective practice, with the express aim of remoulding the past in order to derive a future. This necessitates the implementation of a sifting process capable of reconfiguring and revamping the ideological foundations of the structures which are to be transformed.

In *Reconfiguring Somali Nation*, Abdirachid Mohamed Ismail shows how the Isse Somali managed to snatch victory out of the jaws of defeat. The Isse, along with other groups in the Horn of Africa, endured a painful reordering of society during the 16th century, when Abyssinian forces and their allies defeated the combined forces of the Muslim leader Imam Ahmed Gran, popularly known as Gurey. The defeat led to a deep and disconcerting dispersal of communities. Here, the learned and wise among the Isse sprang into action and drafted a *Xeer* (customary laws), a constitution, to derive the "embryo" (ramparts) of an imagined community (Anderson). The emergence of the Xeer here shares characteristics with similar periods in human history when, as a Somali adage has it, "truth" is created upon the dissolution/disintegration of another truth. The Xeer emerges in the interstitial space/period when the past cannot guide and the future is still in an inchoate stage. This interregnum is rife with contradictions. It is also the period when a simulacrum of order is imagined through myth and fable as well as other elaborate and labyrinthine forms of discursive practice. The ingenuity of the founding fathers of the Xeer lay in their sagacity to view the social ideal as a composite figuration where disparate clans found a home in its grid. Put differently, through the Xeer we witness the narrative strategies by and through which groups in the Isse constellation of clans were forged into an all-encompassing clan-family. Here, the founders understood the syntactic and semiotic connotation of the term "clan" itself. The Somalis say "Tol waa tolane," underlining the basic meaning of the term as "that which is sewn together." The founders were able to imagine a community based on affiliation, not on blood relations. In other words, "Belonging is an act of affiliation and not of birth" (Robert Colls, Geordies: *Roots of Regionalism*, xv). They understood that identity was/is dynamic, dialogic, and protean. Needless to say, these visionaries were "not some illiterate camel herders unaware of international relations and diplomatic affairs" (Abdirachid Mohamed Ismail). In his discussion of the Xeer Isse, Ismail delves into different facets of the Xeer and in the process shows how the Xeer is born of a world much bigger than itself. Here, the author demonstrates by example how the Xeer relates to "education," "experience," "epistemology," and culture as well as human psychology. From there, Ismail extrapolates how the Xeer could be used to help in the construction of a pan-Somali social imagination. This is important in that the author differentiates between what I have called elsewhere "discourses of the nation and discourses of the state." The cultural imaginary developments resulting from such extrapolation will, as the author intimates, assist in the dialectical reconstitution of a new Somali state, whereby the clans and sub-clans will benefit from the Isse experience.

But before that project can become feasible/possible, the author underlines the importance of rethinking some of the categories – that is, general concepts -- through which the Somalis have, over the last several decades, come to apprehend reality. Here, the author pithily explains the pitfalls that have for so long held hostage the construction of a viable national imaginary. This discussion of the national imaginary is fraught with new and daring concepts the likes of which I have not seen/read before. Ismail, for example, calls for a reassessment of the dialectical tussle between such important terms as "unity" and "union." These two terms limn, as I have alluded to elsewhere, the etymology of a conjuncture. Tackling these two terms head-on will assist Somalis surmount the circumstances and events which produced the Somali crisis of the last two or three decades, which led to the death of the supra-nation, the nation that was not meaningfully introjected by the general Somali populace but repeated in overtly ritualized public displays meant to galvanize collective sentiments against real or manufactured external threats. By reflecting the argument of Ismail, such sentiments could be harnessed to produce the requisite discursive formation needed for the clans to become or morph into a nation. One could argue with the drift of some of the points in the author's arguments, even as one cannot doubt his originality and sincerity. One could ask, for example: how does the Xeer apply in a postcolonial, non-harmonized setting which is all the more complicated by the intersection of nation, culture/ethnicityand contending narratives? How do we go about building a new nation in a "post-truth" era where facts vie for prominence with emotion and raw sentiments, doubly complicated by colonially-tampered primordial allegiances? In other words, how do we replicate the success of the Xeer Isse, whose basic tenets were developed synchronously with the moment of defeat, and years before the advent of full-fledged Western colonialism?

Ismail's thesis is full of hope culled from disciplined and methodical thinking. To re-imagine a new collective spirit of a nation built on equality and respect for its constituent parts, Ismail discusses and critically examines the genesis and relevance of the xeer Isse to the current situation. His call is not a wholesale resuscitation of the xeer Isse, as that would ignore the dialectical nature of reality. Neither the times nor the conditions on the ground would favour an application unmediated by wit. Ismail's thesis reminds one of the role of reconnaissance parties whose findings are brought back to the community to ponder and devise ways and means of forging ahead. His examination of the Xeer shows how, in difficult and knotted times, a group of learned individuals pooled their resources and designed a blueprint to help their community extricate itself from a seemingly intractable conundrum. To replicate the feat of the fathers of the Xeer Isse, we must take into consideration Ismail's use of the Somali adage, "*Milil guudkii lama dhayo*" (One does not treat the surface of a suppurating wound/pus). The idea is that thepalliative measures are never a cure. Ismail's book will, no doubt, compel us all to return to the drawing board. His arguments point to new directions, and will in turn help us rethink the Somali conundrum.

Dr. Ali Jimale A. holds an M.A. in African Area Studies and a PhD in Comparative Literature from the University of California, Los Angeles

(UCLA). Poet, cultural critic, short-story writer, and scholar, Jimale is Professor and former chair of Comparative Literature at Queens College of the City University of New York, where he also teaches for the Africana Studies Program and the Department of Classical, Middle Eastern, and Asian Languages and Cultures; he is also on the Comparative Literature faculty at the CUNY Graduate center. His books include *The Invention of Somalia* (1995), *Daybreak Is Near*: Literature, Clansand the Nation-State in Somalia (1996), Fear Is a Cow (2002), *Diaspora Blues* (2005), *The Road Less Traveled*: Reflections on the Literatures of the Horn of Africa (2008, co-edited with the late Taddesse Adera), *When Donkeys Give Birth to Calves*: Totems, Wars, Horizons, Diasporas (2012) and *Gaso, Ganuun iyo Gasiin* (a novel) (2018; roughly translated as "Kraal, Milk, Sustenance"). His poetry and short stories have been translated into several languages, including Japanese, Danish, Bosnian, Portuguese and Turkish.

Dr. Amina Said Chire

L'ouvrage d'Abdirachid Mohamed Ismail constitue un apport réflexif sur la situation de la Somalie. L'entrée retenue pour analyser l'impasse dans laquelle se trouve actuellement ce pays est la culture. Le propos est illustré et enrichi par de nombreuses références bibliographiques.

Dans la première partie de son travail, Abdirachid Mohamed Ismaël (A.M.I) fait un cadrage théorique de son projet éditorial. Cette partie est par conséquent consacrée au concept de culture qui est au centre de son propos.

Ce cadrage théorique lui permet dans une seconde partie d'analyser le rôle de la culture (traditionnelle, islamique, moderne) dans l'échec de l'Etat central somalien via l'analyse du *Somali Union Political Project*. Cette partie est la plus riche et la plus novatrice. Les développements précédents aident à comprendre les raisons profondes de l'échec du SUPP.

Dans cette partie, A.M.I. avance l'hypothèse que le projet de mise en œuvre du concept de « *soomaalinimo* » (SUPP ou Somali Union Political Project) a causé la ruine de l'état central. Pour vérifier cette hypothèse, il remonte le cours de l'Histoire et explore plusieurs pistes.

L'auteur s'attache ainsi à démontrer que le SUPP a causé la ruine de la Somalie selon plusieurs facteurs parmi lesquels il cite
-l'opposition entre le *Somali unity* et le *Somali union*,
-la colonisation qui a tiré profit de l'organisation sociale et territoriale somalie,
-l'ambiguïté du concept de *soomaalinimo* lui-même.
L'auteur analyse en détail chacun de ces facteurs.
Dans un premier temps, il revient sur l'opposition entre le Somali Unity et le SUPP. Il démontre ainsi que le Somali Unity renvoie à la réalité ethnique des Somali, ce qui est pour lui un fait. Il démontre parallèlement que le SUPP est un construit historiquement daté. Rappelons à ce stade de ce compte rendu que le SUPP signifie pour ses partisans l'union dans sous une seule bannière. Et c'est à ce dernier concept qu'A. M. I consacre la majeure partie de sa démonstration.

Dans un deuxième temps, il revient sur le facteur colonial qui a selon lui joué un rôle important dans l'émergence du SUPP. Il rappelle ainsi de quelle manière, les leaders somalis ont tenté d'unir les Somalis sous la même bannière. Le premier de ces leaders est le Sayyid Mohammad Abdillah Hassan qui est d'après l'auteur le premier à tenter d'imposer l'union sous la même bannière, la bannière islamique pour résister à la colonisation de l'espace somali. Ce leader a échoué, car les Somalis ont fini par signer des traités séparés avec des puissances coloniales étrangères.

L'élite somalie post-coloniale a repris le flambeau pour essayer de réaliser l'union. Cette entreprise a également échoué. Pour illustrer son propos, A.M.I rappelle qu'aux élections législatives de 1969, les différents clans somalis ont présenté des représentants. Siyaad Barreh a été le dernier à essayer d'imposer l'union de façon coercitive en important un régime politique étranger aux Somalis, le marxisme léninisme. Son échec fut encore plus retentissant puisque cela a mis fin à l'état central somalien.

Dans un troisième temps, l'auteur explore le rôle de la nature du SUPP dans l'échec de l'Etat central somalien. Pour ce faire, il engage la réflexion dans deux directions. Il démontre ainsi comment le SUPP a monopolisé l'attention au détriment de la construction et de la consolidation de l'Etat central, une situation qui a fragilisé ce dernier. Il renvoie également l'échec du SUPP à sa conception de la construction de l'Etat qui semble être aux antipodes de l'organisation sociale et politique traditionnelle (démocratie pastorale), une raison de plus de l'échec de la greffe. Il conclut par un rappel sur l'origine du SUPP, un projet issu de la vision de l'Elite somalie formée dans des universités étrangères. Cette élite a essayé de d'implémenter le SUPP pour mettre hors d'état de nuire le clan qu'elle considérait comme rétrograde. Les Somalis se sont ainsi battus contre eux-mêmes pour combler le gap entre leur modèle d'organisation socio-politique traditionnelle et le système de gouvernance occidental qu'ils idéalisaient.

Pour sortir de l'impasse et sauver le SUPP, A.M.I propose de repartir sur de nouvelles bases en reconnaissant l'échec du SUPP tel qu'il avait été conçu au départ, en démontrant son importance stratégique pour les Somalis et la stabilité de la région toute entière, en lui donnant un contenu endogène. L'auteur ouvre ainsi quelques perspectives. Il propose de baser le nouveau SUPP sur un projet politique ethnique et une large autonomie des régions avec une priorité absolue accordée aux capacités de résolution des conflits. Il illustre son idée par l'exemple du *xeer ciise*, contrat social permettant entre autres de résoudre les conflits au sein de la confédération clanique du même nom. Il propose même de dupliquer ce contrat social afin de l'appliquer à l'ensemble des Somalis. Si cette démarche étonne un peu, elle ne remet pas en cause la qualité du travail accompli d'A.M.I.

Amina SAID CHIRE is a geographer and professor, specialist in East African nomadism, migration and the risks and vulnerabilities they induce. An expert in urban development and social development for 10 years, she has conducted numerous studies in these two fields (social welfare, gender issues, political and democratic governance, responsible tourism, environmental studies on urban development projects, vulnerability and resilience). She has coordinated and / or participated in the production of reference works on the Republic of Djibouti, including *L'Atlas de Djibouti* (2007), *Djibouti Contemporain* (2012), and *Le Nomade et la ville de Djibouti* (2012). She is presently the head of IRICA (Institut de Recherche Indépendant de la Corne de l'Afrique) and was awarded the Albert Bernard Prize of the French Academy of Sciences of Overseas in 2008 for the *Atlas de Djibouti* and in 2013 for *Le Nomade et la ville de Djibouti*.

Dr. Abdi M. Kusow

Even though Professor Abdirachid M. Ismail mentions the word pragmatic only once in the entire text, it is clear from his theoretical comments that his use of the word is rooted in a wider pragmatist philosophy. My purpose in this short reflection is to build on the theoretical outline presented in the "New Insights on Culture..." by suggesting pragmatism as a possible philosophical basis for conceptualizing this moment in the social and political history of Somali society. In the sense of the usual terminologies which could be observed on a daily basis, pragmatism refers to "an approach that assesses the truth of meaning of theories or beliefs in terms of the success of their practical applications."

In the Somali context, it could be observed that in a similar manner with any other idea, the Somali Union Political Project (SUPP) is not an inherent property, except in the consequences which it produces for the Somali society in the Horn of Africa. And on that score, we can say that it failed in its practical application, and if anything, produced a disastrous outcome for the entire Somali society. It is therefore fair to assume that the Somali Union Political Project was not and is not, an empirically conceived conceptor at least, as Professor Ismail pointed out, the history that the Somali elite told about the project which did not correspond to the empirical reality on the ground.

They have, in other words constructed the story of the project on a greater Somalia based on, not what is, but what it ought to be, or what I otherwise refer to as the theoretical versus the empirical Somali.

The theoretical story Somali elites constructed depicted the society as a self-same nation, and downplays, and sometimes violently oppresses any mention of social and political faultlines. The only acknowledged political and social faultlines, according to self-same nation thesis, are those that resulted from Faragelin Shisheeye (foreign intervention) otherwise colonialism both European and what Somalis habitually refer to Gumaysiga Madow (black colonists). If colonial actors are not blamed, moreover, the breakdown of the Somali moral fiber, according to the self-same nation thesis, could be traced to the actions of one or another post-colonial regime, which allegedly pitted hitherto harmonious and homogeneous clans against each otherand thereby, destroyed the cultural and spiritual values of the society leading to the present crisis. More importantly, this historiography articulates the making of the Somali nation as the result of the Darwiish anti-colonial resistance movement which supposedly rescued the nation from the British overlords, while conveniently ignoring the founder of the Qadiriyya Movement, Shaykh Uways B. Muhammad Al-Barawi (aka Shiekh Uways Biyooleyyaale) who not only led a Somali anti-colonial resistance movement, but also an East African, particularly anti-German colonialism movement in southern Tanganyika. The irony here is that Sayid Mohamed Abdullah Hassan himself incited his followers against Shaykh Uways, who ambushed and killed the Shaykh in 1909 in Biyooleey, Bakool region, undermining at once the most significant anti colonial movement in the region.

The empirical Somali story, on the other hand is based on a Somali society consisting of host of intersecting cultural and economic identities raging from settled agriculture, dryland farming, agro-pastoralism, fishing, to cow-based, goat-based, and camel-based Nomadism. Unlike what the theoretical story tends to tell us, the mode of economic production,that a particular clan leads is not necessarily based on geographic or spatial location. For example, agriculture is practiced in every region of the country from the northwest, west, southand southwest. Again, beside the theoretical story, one of the most extensive camel-based nomadic cultures is practiced in the Bakool region of the southwest, rather than at the central Mudug region.

This empirical Somali story, moreover, is culturally diverse and consists of communities which speak multiple languages and dialects which include a Banadir Coast Kiswahili and a variety of Somali languages that include Jiiddu and Garre. More importantly, within the country, particularly in southern Somalia, two primary Somali dialects, *Maay and Maxaa*, are spoken with the Shebelle River as the dividing line. The Maay dialect is the Lingua Franca for the overwhelming majority of the inhabitants situated at the south of the Shebelle River, while the *Maxaa* is Lingua Franca for the populations north of the Shebelle Riverand of course, the official national language. Whether Maay is a dialect or a language is beside the point, we know that the two languages, dialects are unintelligible with each other and beyond that, the Maay dialect serves as a cultural identity for a significant segment of the population.

The most important aspect of the empirical Somaliand, the one which the theoretical Somali story tends to put under the carpet, is the existence of a fundamental system of social stratification and inequality. The Somali social structure acknowledges three major minority groups: 1) the Somali Bantu/Jareer; 2) TheBandadiri/Reer Hamarand 3) The occupational caste groups, such as Gabooye, Tumal, Yibir and Midgaan.

The idea of social inequality is not just limited to the minority groups, but occurs within the so-called four major clan groups and within the regional states as well. Here the theoretical narrative tells us that the regional states were created through a bottom-up processand they are primarily divided along single clan lines. The empirical narrative on the ground, however, tells a different story. That story is that almost all regions contain multiple different clans, but one or two clans primarily dominate each regional state and the rest feel socially, politically and economically alienated.

Beyond the nature of inequality, the boundary between the regional states is not very clearly demarcated and agreed upon as in the cases between Somaliland and Puntland and between Southwest and Jubbaland. It is important to note also, that some of the regional states, particularly, Jubbaland, was not created through a bottom-up decision-making process.

The current historical movement is contrary to the greater Somalia dream that portrayed the Somali society moving from sub-national and local identities to Pan-Somalia identity, when in fact it took a reverse process that accentuates more conflicted localized identities which have, if unchecked, the potential to turn Somalia into several regional client states. This brings us to the question, where to from here? The answer is to dialectically understand and simultaneously overcome both the locally driven societal forces and the regional geopolitical and demographic forces whichhave collectively contributed to the disintegration of the Somali Union Political Project (SUPP). I underline both dialectical and simultaneity because the two forces do not behave in linear fashion. It is sort of the chicken-egg situation. At any rate, the Somali society has to embrace the equality clause of the Somali-Issa Xeer, *Ciise waa Ciise* ("Issa is an Issa"), and truly embrace a "Soomaali waa Soomaali, in the real sense of the word, but not in the military regime style of burring Clannism and using it in back-handed way at the same time. This is very important because despite what the theoretical Somali story tells, the most fundamental issue that underlies the Somali political crisis is inequality and the lack of acceptance of the multiple voices and identities which constitutethe idea of Somaliness. The process requires going beyond the theoretical story to understand the actual distribution of the different clanswhich live in every regional state, not just the politically powerful ones. And at any rate, the current political culture based on the dubious Four-Point-Five power sharing mechanism must be eliminated altogether.

The second set of issues which require a clear understanding is the geopolitical and demographic transformation that is occurring in the region. The Somali society must move away from the Somali Union Political Project as articulated in the theoretical story and embrace an empirically driven one, one that assesses the integralcomparative advantage demographically, economically and militarily in relation to neighboring countries. The Somali society, in other words, must understand the integration of forces which are sweeping the region. Its pragmatic outcome notwithstanding, the recent joint press conference between the Ethiopian Prime Minister, Abiy Ahmed and the Somali President, Mohamed Abdullahi Mohamed in Villa Somalia, which literally occurred as I was writing, is a clear sign of what will unfold in the region in the next 20 years. Again, before Somalis are able to become a core state in the region and are able to dictate its strategic interest, it must construct a Somali nation where every individual and every Juffo truly could feel that they are part of the nation, *Soomaali waa Soomaali, cidna cid, caaro ma dheera.*

Finally, without necessarily providing a blue print here, I also see the necessity of the self-determination of the Somaliland territory, but only in such a way that does not weaken the collective strategy of the Somali region. The idea is unless that collective strategic and comparative advantage could be preserved, all regions including Somaliland will ultimately become client city-states to Ethiopia.

And for Mogadishu to become the true "incubator and the catalyst of the ideal Somali Nation," It must be imagined, not as a regional idea, but as a national space. It should be considered that the demography of the greater Mogadishu area consisted of people from multiple clans which hail from middle Shebelle, Southwest and significant number of Somali

Bantu/Jarweerwayne, Banadiri people, etc. In any case, to imagining Mogadishu as a national space is to allow all its citizens to elect their leaders through a one-person-one vote system and that is ultimately the only meaningful way to imagine a new Somalia with Mogadishu as the true incubator.

Dr. Abdi M. Kusow is Professor of Sociology at Iowa State University. He is an internationally recognized sociologist in immigration and socioeconomic integration among immigrants. Professor Kusow is also a recognized scholar on the social and geopolitical dynamics of the Horn of Africa region. His research appeared in top ranked sociology and international migration journals and serves as an editorial board member on leading sociology journals. Professor Kusow has given invited keynote speeches at many national and international universities, including Ohio State University, Aalborg University, Denmark, York University, Canadaand Sun Yat-sen University, Guangzhou, Chinaand the Doha Forum. Professor Kusow is Co-editor of the *Journal of Somali Studies* (JoSS).

Fowsia Abdulkadir

It is always interesting to read books about Somalia's socio-political culture and more so when it could be written by a Somali author. Abdirachid M. Ismail's book provides an interdisciplinary perspective on Somali culture and brings fresh insights into the notion of Somalinimo or Somaliness. In this book, Ismail attempts to discern *Somalinimo* or "Somaliness" from historically dominant narratives, in essence, writing about Somali culture from a Somali vintage point.

Section One

In the first part of this book, Ismail unpacks the concept of culture and its multiple definitions employing various approaches across disciplines and delving into Anthropology, Sociology, Psychology and Biology perspectives, highlighting each of contributions of these approaches.Ismail critically analyses theories on culture highlighting these as "an integrated whole" which could permit humans to cope with environmental challenges and build resilience. He underscores "culture as means to survive" and "culture as a process of attaining a better state of being". To elaborate on these aspects of culture, the author, further, unpacks what he terms the basic constituents of culture, i.e., environment, education and experience, leading to understanding of the various stages of Ken Wilber's theory of "Integral Culture" where human societies pass through four phases (egocentric; ethnocentric; worldcentric and a final stage of integration). In other words, the author posits that culture is dynamic and allows people to enhance their faculties (physical, mental and spiritual). What is interesting about this theoretical construct section is that the discussion on the variations in culture could lead to the building of an understanding of a continuum "towards a culture of spirit", which is a holistic approach to the evolution of societal culture.

Section Two

In the second section, the author contributes to the larger discussion and/or narratives on how did Somalia get here and attempts to peel layers of tumultuous history ripe with contradictions. What is refreshing about Ismail's contribution is that his perspective is anchored in the concept of Somalinimo rooted in Somali "Xeer-dhaqameed: traditional law".

Ismail introduces a concept he calls "The Somali Unity Political Project" and its evolution over the decades. The author highlights some historical differences in how this concept of "Somali Unity Political Project" has been portrayed over the years by Somalis and non-Somalis underlining how these different portrayals might have created ongoing "discordance and disharmony".[174] The author argues that to move the conversation forward, from divergent narratives, while building on these somewhat contradicting historical perspectives, is to reinforce the notion of Soomaalinimo which is an informal but powerful concept among Somalis across the Somali territories. Ismail proposes that reviving this concept of Soomaalinimo through the prism of Somali heritage "Xeer-dhaqameed or traditional law" will provide a much needed paradigm shift in the Somali socio-political discourse. Here the author invokes a Somali saying "*hanta gunta ayaa laga tolaa* -ama – *Haani guntay ka tolantaa*", (a wooden bucket is sawn from the bottom), which in essence means you need to secure the base or the foundation on which you are building or one needs to build on a solid foundation.

Also in this section, the author provides a lengthy discussion on how the Somali Unity Political Project failed and how this failure is linked across some historical continuities, illustrated through the struggle of the Somalis for independence and the total collapse of the Somali State. Ismail highlights few factors such as, at first, distinguishing between "Somali unity" and "Somali Union". Here the author differentiates the ethnic reality in the Somali territories (Somali unity))and the historical political project (Somali Union).)Secondly, the colonization factor and its aftermath is discussedand thirdly, the ambiguity and/or abstractedness of the concept of Soomaalinimo is analysed, which, according to the author, worked as a mobilizing factor during the struggle for independence.

Section Three

In this section, the author presents an interesting and somewhat ambitious forward looking proposal, terming it "the new project", "that is not intended to declare war on neighbouring states to (not) recapture lost territories, but, to put in place the structure that allows the nation to maintain its cultural and linguistic cohesion, to consider its shared destiny as a community and to consolidate stability and peace in the Horn of African".

I think this is an innovative thinking, however, as a very ambitious one as it calls for a new Somali Union Project contingent on what the author considers to be four major principles statements:
It should not mean the disunion of any other nation and should not be done against any nation.
It should not need to be recognized by others and should be based on undisputable facts.
It should be in concord with Somali secular traditional laws.
It should be in concord with international laws.
As I have stated at the beginning of this review, this was an interesting manuscript to read, it brings newer perspectives on culture and the Somali socio-political culture in particular. The Arguments of Ismail are grounded in the importance of how Somali Xeer-dhaqameed is valued and perceived by all Somalis across the Somali inhabited territories. It is an ambitious forward looking thought provoking concept which calls for a paradigm shift. Reflection on this idea, however, brings to mind this question:

Can Somalis reach that harmonized unified cohesion in the Horn of Africa while still living in geographically and political separated countries? In my opinion, this is an important question to move the conversation forward, given the current context of the Somali State and Somali inhabited territories.

Ms. Abdulkadir is an independent researcherand human rights activist. Her research interests can be placed in the international and Canadian national arenas. In the international context, her research interests are in the areas of conflict analysis, transitional justice or post conflict justice mechanisms, gender mainstreaming and the role of women in governance, democratization and conflict resolution in the Horn of Africa. Current research projects include transitional justice in the context of Somalia's failed statehood. In the Canadian national context, her research interests are in Canadian social policy analysis and public sector accountability.

Dr. Hamdi Mohamed

The Somali saying *"nin bukaa boqol u talisay"* ("a sick man has hundred sorts of advices") characterizes the current Somali challenge. So many "solutions" have been proposed to deal with the political and social crises since 1990s. The common feature of most of these so-called solutions is that they are externally driven. In fact, having been living, learning and working in Somalia in the past five years, I have witnessed a peculiar phenomenon of people (mostly the elites) who are willing to embrace anything foreign while shunning indigenous culture, wisdoms and ideas. For the younger generation, the unwillingness to learn from the experiences of the older generation is understandable, as they tend to be exposed to and sometimes inculcate the dominant negative and stereotypical narrative about Somalia and Somalis.

The book's recognition of the fundamental need for "a new way of looking at things" is particularly apropos in this context where anything foreign is valued and everything Somali is pathologized. I enjoyed reading it and found it provocative, passionate and informative - contributing to our knowledge and understanding of who we are as people in a number of specific ways. First, the suggestion to "go back to the dark places where we have lost the key" proposes a new methodological approach. This approach is timely and necessary to move forward on our efforts to find solutions which could be grounded in Somali knowledge, cultural values, in the collective wisdom of our ancestors and within our experiences.

Second, the principle *"haanta gunta ayaa laga tolaa"*, which I found myself to have quoted quite often in public speeches in Somalia and Kenya, is powerful and speaks to the importance of addressing underlying complex issues of governance and state-building instead of the symptoms. The in-depth and historical mapping of the traditional systems of governance and institutions is a foundational and necessary step towards the suitable articulation and development of a "new paradigm about Somaliness".

Third, the supra-clanic segment (CSCS) the potential to "open a new chapter of Somali history" is hopeful, inspiring and definitely worth exploring further. Inviting a larger and public conversation and debates on this will move beyond the "imported systems of governance which are poorly suited for the Somali cultural and political context" - creating more space for credible local democratic processes.

Finally, while this book is one of the most valuable works on Somalia and Somalis I have read recently, it is not clear why there is no discussion on Islam. I find the focus on "secular Somali traditions" curious and it creates a gap and weakens the book's contribution to the development of a holistic understanding of the issues under discussion.

Dr. Hamdi Mohamed is a social historian with multidisciplinary skills and experiences in issues of Africa and African Diaspora. She is the author of Gender and the" Politics of Nation Building: (Re)Constructing Somali Women's History" and several other books and journal articles. Her teaching and research interest areas include women and politics, international migration, gender and development, research methodology and indigenous knowledge systems.

She has been leading major national applied research and results-based monitoring and evaluation projects in Somalia with a specific focus on social research designs, methodologies, inquiry frameworks and linking research to policy and practice in the past several years. She has a wide range of university teaching experiences in North America and Africa and lectured widely on issues of social policy, international development, gender and politics as well as on human rights.

Zaynab A. Sharci

Somalis and friends of Somalis have enjoyed Dr Abdirachid M Ismail's extensive academic work. The topic we have here has somewhat differed from the path we have come to associate with Ismail.

A powerful argument is well articulated replete with enlightening references. It forces you to 'listen' and pay attention. It demands one's attention and comprehension and evokes feelings of patriotism and loyalty to Somaliness. Is it not food for thought whilst there is this mistrust, scepticism and 'enmity' between Somalia, Ethiopia and Kenya, backed or not by their allies, are trying their best to reinforce their positions as core nations in the Horn of Africa?

After twenty eight years, can we dare to imagine a peaceful Horn of Africa? Is it a pipe dream? Is it a possibility? After digesting the contents of this work, it is another question for the reader to perceive.

The preamble to Ismail's work focuses on culture where the author theorises a concept he names E3. I feel that the message within this concept needs to be studied well, learnt from and utilised. At thispoint, I arrived at another question: Are the Somalis of today ready for this message, is the environment conducive to contribute to the essence of this work and are Somalis tired (from the experience) of the same old story of tribalism, hunger for power, lack of empathy for the other etc. ?

The book is an addictive read from whatever spectrum one could conform to, politically or socially. The work envisages a historical restart, wounds to be healed in order to achieve reconciliation and peace. I imagine the work or the 'environment' critically need great inspiring leaders to precipitate, who could be immune to greed and ambition for any coveted seat, similar to that of the Nelson Mandela of South Africa.

Ismail's convincing persuasion is about peace and reconciliation and here, another question arises for me. Has this work arrived at the right time? A time where the gulf of testing each other's waters is at a high. Only time will reveal the outcomes.

Although I am not politically inclined towards any specific philosophy or approach, nevertheless, in Ismail's powerful citations and reasoning, I have gone through a rollercoaster of emotions and thoughts. The work entices and draws one in without one's awareness. One interacts with the cleverly woven script, demanding a response from a non-living entity. I believe and hope this conversation with Ismail's work will continue and bring forth the answers its readers demand.

Finally, I found the work a bold and sincere move, Ismail's first book deviating from the work which he is renowned for, daring to advice politicians and their public. Whatever path Somali politicians lead their people to, Dr Ismail has done his moral duty by committing his thoughts and heart through putting pen to paper and by formulating a record for history to witness and refer to.

Zaynab A. Sharci is the founder of *Galool, Home of Somali Education & Resources* and the author of Somali-English learning resources for Somalis in the diaspora. Saynab, who, until recently, was a deputy head teacher at a UK secondary school as well as a community activist in the UK, now resides in Hargeysa so that she may continue what she calls 'her self-imposed campaign and personal legacy for her community'. Her interest in Somali grammar and fascination with Somali culture in general, allows her to develop deeper understanding of issues such as identity and defines her literary works.

[174] "The postulate behind this interpretation of events is that man makes history. Our assumption, however, is that nature makes history and man tells stories about it, and we will try to show how, through the concept of *"the Somali Unity Political Project"* (labelled SUPP here) and its evolution.

INDEX

A

Abdalla O. Mansur, 78, 86
Abdi M. Kusow, iv
Abdikarim Sheick Muuse, 67
Abdisalam M. Issa-Salwe, 50, 79, 82
Abyssinian, 59, 117
adaptation, 37, 39, 41, 83, 102
Africa, 50, 64, 75, 80, 82, 84, 86, 87, 88, 95, 108, 112, 113, 131, 132
Ahmed I. Samatar, 47, 48, 78, 79
Ali Jimale A., iv, 47
Alter-ego, 34
Amina S. Chiré, iv
animal, 16, 21, 37, 40, 41, 49, 103
anthropology, 11, 13, 47, 111
Anthropology, 12, 15, 20, 35, 36, 39, 43, 44, 127
Aout, 11
Arabs, 105
archetype, 32
Arnold Matthew, 13
art, 11, 16, 17, 38, 41
artistic, 16, 38, 39
astrology, 104, 106
Atkinson, 28, 46
awareness, 24, 33, 34, 132

B

barbarism, 13, 14
basic constituents, 20, 128
Beck, 41, 42, 44
behaviors, 20, 39

beliefs, 11, 14, 17, 18, 20, 41, 123
Benda, 34
Benedict, 31
Berbera, 59, 72, 85, 88, 96
Bevin, 60, 73
Biology, 12, 13, 49, 127
bipedalism, 36
Blakemore, 13
Boas, 13, 44
Bonner, 21, 45
Bosaaso, 90
bottom-up, 91, 93, 107, 125
Bucur Bacayr, 51
Building Block, 90
Bulhan, 91

C

Cabdalla Xaaji, 102
Cabdiraxmaan C. Faarax, "Barwaqo, 50
Campbell, 35
cannibalism, 35
Caraweelo, 51
Cassanelli, 71, 72, 85
cell, 21, 23, 26, 29, 110
cellular, 22, 23, 28, 29
central government, 48, 52, 64
centralized, 58, 67, 68, 69, 70, 71, 76, 92, 107, 109
China, 52, 55, 56
choice, 35, 37
civilization, 13, 16, 30, 39
Civilization and its discontents, 31, 44

clan, 48, 52, 53, 56, 58, 61, 63, 66, 67, 68, 69, 70, 72, 78, 83, 84, 88, 90, 99, 100, 102, 104, 106, 107, 108, 109, 110, 114, 118, 124, 125
clannism, 47, 53, 67, 70, 71, 91, 92
clanship, 91
Clash of Civilizations, viii
cognitive, 39, 40
colonization, 14, 56, 57, 58, 59, 60, 61, 73, 74, 88, 105, 107, 108, 129
competition, 33, 36, 52, 54, 55, 56, 58, 88, 93, 101
Conflict Resolution Capacity, 90, 93, 113, 116
consciousness, 22, 23, 24, 30, 31, 34, 39, 41, 42, 50, 59, 68
constitution, 31, 61, 64, 70, 77, 97, 99, 100, 107, 108, 109, 117
cooperation, 33, 36, 81
core nation, 51, 96, 99
Core-Periphery Theory, 96
corruption, 52, 53, 67, 91, 92, 113
Cosmices, 35
cosmogonic, 39
Cowan, 41, 42
CRC, 113, Voir Conflit Resolution Capacity
creativity, 17, 38, 93
CSCS. Voir Supra-Clannic Segment
Cuba, 75, 76

cultural, vii, 13, 14, 18, 19, 20, 21, 26, 35, 36, 39, 40, 41, 43, 44, 54, 69, 70, 82, 84, 87, 99, 106, 107, 108, 111, 114, 118, 120, 123, 124, 129, 131
cultural stages, 40
culture, vi, vii, viii, ix, 11, 12, 13, 14, 15, 16, 17, 18, 19, 20, 21, 23, 24, 25, 27, 28, 29, 30, 31, 33, 34, 36, 37, 38, 39, 40, 41, 42, 43, 44, 45, 47, 50, 57, 58, 60, 110, 111, 118, 119, 124, 126, 127, 129, 130, 132, 133
Culture, vii, viii, 11, 15, 16, 18, 20, 26, 30, 31, 34, 35, 42, 44, 45, 110, 123, 128
customary, 57, 58, 78, 89, 99, 100, 102, 117

D

Daraawiish, 56, 79
Darwin, 14, 18
Darwinism, 15, 35
Dawkins, vii, 13, 14, 18, 19, 20, 26, 35
de Chardin, 41, 42, 49, 50
democracy, 67, 91, 114
democratic, 27, 48, 52, 71, 90, 96, 114, 131
Dennett, 13
Dervish, 68, 72, 77, 105, 106
determinism, 17, 50
dhaqan, vi, vii, viii
dictatorship, 48, 67, 71
dilemma, 25, 92, 111

divination, 104
Djibouti, iv, vi, 52, 60, 62, 63, 64, 65, 66, 75, 76, 78, 79, 80, 81, 82, 88, 97, 109, 115
Djibouti,, 115
DNA, 22
DP Word, 88

E

ecological setting, 14, 15
ecology, 22, 90
economic, viii, 16, 27, 28, 54, 64, 71, 81, 96, 107, 113, 114, 124
economic imperatives, viii
Economy, 15, 112, 113
education, vii, 20, 26, 27, 28, 38, 39, 40, 68, 72, 80, 110, 118, 128
ego, 31, 33, 34, 51
Ego, 31, 33, 34
Elders, 59, 102, 115
elitist, 13, 14, 15, 23, 27
emancipation, 41
embryonic, 36, 52
Emirates, 56, 81
energy, 21
environment, 14, 16, 18, 20, 21, 23, 25, 26, 27, 28, 29, 30, 36, 37, 39, 41, 43, 45, 83, 99, 100, 110, 111, 113, 128, 132
equality, 94, 102, 103, 119, 125
Ethiopia, 51, 55, 56, 58, 63, 64, 65, 67, 71, 73, 74, 75, 76, 78, 83, 88, 96, 97, 98, 99, 105, 109, 110, 112, 113, 126, 132

ethnic, 54, 55, 57, 58, 61, 63, 65, 66, 74, 76, 83, 89, 99, 107, 109, 112, 114, 129
ethnocentrism, 14, 92
ethology, 13, 20
Europe, vi
Evolution of Species theory, 13
experience, 18, 26, 28, 29, 30, 31, 33, 37, 39, 48, 84, 90, 110, 118, 128, 132
experimentation, 26, 28

F

family, vi, vii, 21, 22, 25, 28, 83, 94, 100, 104, 108, 111, 118
Fascism, 14
Federal State of Somalia, 61, 66, 67, 88, 89, 93, 94, 95, 97, 98, 99, 107
federal system, 48
Finkerkraut, 17
Fitzgibbon, 60
France, 59, 115
French Somali Coast. Voir Djibouti
Freud, 16, 30, 31, 44
FSS. Voir Federal State of Somalia

G

Gande, 102
Geertz, 35
genes, 18, 19, 20, 36, 44, 45
genetic, 19, 26, 33, 37

geography, 21
geostrategic, 96, 97, 107
Geshekter, 72
global, iv, viii, 15, 23, 25, 27, 31, 42, 43, 49, 50, 78, 83, 91, 111
God, 24, 103, 104
Goodenough, 31
governance, 21, 39, 48, 53, 67, 69, 71, 78, 84, 90, 92, 94, 96, 99, 106, 112, 113, 130, 131
Graves, 42
Guddi, 102, 105, 115
guilty, 106

H

Haile Selassie, 75
harmony, 22, 38
Hassan Gouled Aptidon, 76
Haud, 59, 73
Hegel, 50
Herder, 14
Herodotus, 14
hierarchy, 13, 16, 39
historiography, 48, 50, 52, 124
history, viii, ix, 34, 44, 48, 49, 50, 51, 52, 53, 54, 56, 57, 64, 67, 78, 80, 83, 85, 88, 89, 98, 108, 109, 114, 117, 123, 128, 131, 133, 134
holistic, 49, 79, 128, 131
homogeneity, 22, 63
Horjooge, 102
Horn. Voir Horn of Africa
Horn of Africa, iv, 51, 60, 61, 64, 74, 82, 87, 88, 89, 95, 97, 101, 107, 110, 113, 114, 117, 120, 123, 127, 130, 132
human, vii, viii, 11, 12, 13, 14, 15, 16, 17, 18, 19, 20, 21, 22, 25, 26, 27, 28, 30, 31, 33, 34, 35, 36, 37, 38, 39, 40, 41, 42, 47, 49, 50, 82, 103, 117, 128, 130, 131
humanity, viii, 28
Huxley, 42
hymenopteran, 36

I

Ibraahim Axmad Cali, 102, 115
Ibrahim Moallin Mursal, 69
ideas, 11, 12, 14, 17, 18, 28, 31, 75, 78, 98, 130
identities, viii, 124, 125
Imam Ahmed Gran, 117
independence, 53, 59, 60, 62, 64, 65, 66, 67, 69, 70, 71, 73, 74, 82, 84, 90, 96, 129
Indian Ocean, 88, 98, 114
indigenous, 43, 60, 69, 70, 96, 98, 107, 130, 131
individual, 17, 21, 25, 33, 36, 37, 38, 39, 42, 51, 53, 61, 111, 126
individuality, 33, 34, 39
individuation, 32, 33, 39, 40
Information, 21, 27
instinct, 25, 111
institutional, 23
integrated, 18, 41, 42, 50, 66, 127
intellectuals, 13, 58, 70, 78, 90

intelligence, 15, 24
intelligent design theory, 24
interaction, 25, 105, 111
international competitions, 88
IRICA, iv
Islamic, 57, 68, 72, 77, 88, 93, 94, 111, 112, 116
Islamic Courts, 94, 112
Issa, iv, 50, 79, 82, 100, 101, 102, 103, 105, 106, 109, 114, 125
Italia, 69, 73
Italian, 61, 62, 64, 68, 73, 74
Iye, 100, 101, 102, 104, 106, 114, 115, 116

J

Jaamac C. Isse, 50, 79
Jigjiga, 57
jihad, 56, 59, 81
Jimale. Voir Ali Jimale A.
Jubaland, 51
Jung, 31, 32, 33, 39, 46
Jungian, 32, 40

K

Kant, 17, 44
Kenya, 51, 55, 56, 62, 63, 64, 65, 73, 74, 83, 96, 98, 99, 109, 114, 131, 132
King, 100, 102, 103, 104, 106, 109
Kluckhohn, 11, 12, 41, 44

knowledge, iv, 11, 15, 16, 20, 25, 26, 27, 28, 29, 31, 37, 38, 39, 40, 50, 52, 105, 111, 130, 131
Kritarchy, 67
Kroeber, 11, 12, 44

L

Laitin, 57, 64, 81
language, vii, 35, 50, 57, 114, 124
law, 16, 31, 36, 48, 57, 58, 59, 69, 70, 72, 78, 91, 94, 100, 102, 103, 106, 128
laws, 11, 22, 70, 87, 91, 94, 99, 110, 114, 117, 129
layers, 22, 23, 26, 32, 128
learning, 29, 35, 36, 39, 46, 133
Lestel, 36
Lévi-Strauss, 13, 18, 44
Lewis, 44, 47, 59, 67, 68, 69, 71, 74, 82, 84, 85, 90, 91, 112
liberation, 68, 76
Lilius, 59, 60, 82
linguistic, 35, 84, 87, 99, 129
Linton, 41
living being, 16, 25, 31, 33, 34, 37, 40, 111
local, vii, viii, 23, 28, 59, 72, 90, 92, 125, 131
love, 30, 113
Lowell, 11, 43
Lumsden, viii, 18

M

macroscopic, 22

Mahrer, 37, 46
Malinowski, 16, 17, 18, 19, 23, 28, 36, 41, 44
Maslow, 30, 36, 37
matriliny, 35
matrix, 29
Matsumoto, 20, 45
Matsuzawan, 21
Maxamad Nuur Galaal, 75
Mayr, 42
mechanical, 22, 29, 30, 36, 40, 41
medicinal, 39
medium, 21, 22, 23, 66
Meles Zenawi, 76, 98
membership, 36
meme, 19
memes, 18, 19, 20, 44
memory, 26, 33, 34, 46, 56
Menelik, 58, 73
Mengistu Haile Mariam, 76
Mercier, 35
Merka, 57
microscopic, 20, 21, 33
militia, 53, 94
mimetic, 35, 40, 41
Mohamed Omar Osman, 73
molecular biology, 13, 14
monolithic, 43
Montesquieu, 51
Moqadisho, 61, 87, 94, 95
morals, 11
Morgan, 13, 16
Morin, 21
morphogenetic, 40
Muslim, 105, 114, 117

N

natural state, 13, 78, 87
Nazism, 14
neo-Darwinians, 14
Neo-Darwinist, 13
nepotism, 52, 53, 67, 70, 84, 91
NFD, 62, 63, 64, 73, 74
Notten, 67, 84, 90
nucleus, 21, 23, 26, 87

O

Ogaden, 59, 73, 74, 75
Omar. O. Rabeh, 49
organism, 29, 33, 45, 49, 110
organization, 22, 23, 36, 48, 58, 67, 68, 70, 71, 77, 91, 92, 99, 100, 102, 112
otherness, 30

P

Pan-Africanism, 75
Pan-Somali Movement, 69
paradigm, 27, 39, 43, 48, 128, 129, 131
paradox, 57, 66, 108
pastoral, 21, 57, 67, 68, 100, 106, 108, 114
patronage, 91, 107
peace, 53, 59, 87, 91, 93, 112, 114, 129, 132
pendulum, 99
peripheral nation, 51
personality, 33
pole, 29

policy, 19, 53, 63, 65, 69, 79, 91, 93, 96, 98, 105, 113, 130, 131
Primal, 36
primitive, 17, 20, 21, 38, 39, 70, 105
Protagoras, 14
psychic, 22, 30, 31
psychology, vii, 12, 13, 15, 20, 25, 30, 31, 35, 40, 46, 118, 127
Psychology, 45, 78, 79, 83
Puntland, 66, 90, 125

Q

Qalbi Dhagax. Voir Abdikarim Sheuck Muuse
Qatar, 56

R

Radcliffe-Brown, 11, 43
Red Sea, 81, 86, 88, 98
Redfield, 41, 43
Redfield Robert, 11
refinement, 33, 39
relativism, 13, 14, 50
religion, 16, 41, 43
Rendell, 21, 45
Renders, 70, 90
representations, viii, 39
reproduction, 17, 18, 36
Republic of Somalia, 64, 65
Reserved Area, 73
resilience, 15, 16, 17, 18, 28, 127
resistance, 59, 85, 124

resources, 16, 22, 59, 80, 85, 86, 87, 88, 101, 119, 133
revolution, 24
rudimentary, 39
rules, 22, 67, 70, 71, 92, 94, 96, 103, 104

S

Sagal M. Djama, 102
Said Samatar, 57, 58, 81
Samatar. Voir Ahmed I. Samatar
Sapir, 13
Saudi Arabia, 56, 75, 111
savages, 35
Sayid Mohamed Abdalla Hassan, 58, 59, 71, 105
Sayid Mohamed Abdallah Hassan, 50, 56, 72, 77
scholars, 11, 13, 18, 48, 69, 90, 96, 112, 114
school, vi, 27, 28, 68, 133
science, 25, 29, 43
Self, 32, 33, 34, 41
self-consciousness, 30, 32, 37
Selfish Gene, vii, 18, 20
self-preservation, 25, 27, 111
Shabelle Rivers, 98
Sheik Hassan, 69
Shiffrin, 28, 46
shift, 18, 61, 111, 128, 129
Simpson, 42
Sisyphus, 99, 114
Siyad. Voir Siyad Barre
Siyad Barre, 48, 53, 58, 70, 71, 76, 77, 112

skill, 11
Slight, 50, 79, 82, 85
socialization, 36
sociobiology., viii
sociology, 12, 13, 15, 20, 49, 127
Socrates, 52
Somali, iv, vi, vii, viii, ix, 47, 48, 49, 51, 52, 53, 54, 55, 56, 57, 58, 59, 60, 61, 62, 63, 64, 65, 66, 67, 68, 69, 70, 71, 72, 73, 74, 75, 76, 77, 78, 79, 80, 81, 82, 83, 84, 85, 86, 87, 88, 89, 90, 91, 92, 93, 94, 95, 96, 97, 98, 99, 100, 101, 102, 103, 105, 106, 107, 108, 109, 110, 111, 112, 114, 116, 117, 118, 119, 123, 124, 125, 126, 127, 128, 129, 130, 131, 133, 134
Somali Union, 57, 58, 60, 61, 63, 77, 87, 123, 125, 126, 129
Somali Unity Political Project. SUPP
Somalia, ix, 48, 51, 52, 53, 54, 60, 61, 63, 64, 65, 66, 67, 68, 69, 72, 73, 74, 75, 76, 77, 78, 79, 80, 81, 82, 83, 84, 85, 86, 88, 90, 92, 93, 94, 97, 98, 101, 107, 108, 109, 112, 113, 114, 116, 120, 123, 124, 125, 126, 127, 128, 130, 131, 132
Somaliland, vi, 51, 62, 64, 65, 66, 68, 69, 73, 80, 81, 84, 90, 91, 95, 96, 97, 98, 99, 107, 109, 110, 112, 115, 125, 126
somaliness. Voir soomaalinimo
somalinism. Voir soomaalinimo

soomaalinimo, 54, 57, 58, 60, 61, 63, 66, 68
Soutenelle, 38
Southern Somalia, 98
South-West State, 66
Soviet Union, 73, 75, 76
Spencer, 11, 13
spiritual, 16, 17, 27, 34, 38, 42, 72, 124, 128
stability, 87, 94, 129
Steiner, 60, 82
SUPER, 90, 91, 94, 99, 107, 109, 110
superego, 31, 34
superiority, 14, 39
Super-Self, 32, 33
SUPP, 48, 54, 57, 58, 61, 63, 64, 65, 66, 67, 68, 69, 70, 71, 72, 73, 74, 75, 76, 77, 78, 87, 97, 99, 100, 107, 123, 125, 134
Supra-Clannic Segment, 108, 109
Suzanne Lilius, iv, 60, 79, 82
SYL, 54, 58, 69
symbol, 19, 56
system, 12, 14, 15, 19, 20, 22, 23, 26, 27, 36, 46, 48, 52, 66, 69, 70, 71, 75, 77, 78, 90, 91, 92, 93, 94, 96, 108, 112, 125, 127
systemic, 49

T

Taylor, 13, 112
technics, 11, 19
terrain, 23

territory, 22, 54, 55, 59, 61, 63, 65, 66, 67, 73, 74, 76, 82, 92, 93, 95, 96, 97, 98, 99, 109, 116, 126
TFAI, 60, 63, 64
theoretical reflection, ix
Tilikaninen, vi
Tooby, 35
tradition, 36, 47, 58, 100, 117
transformation, 23, 30, 39, 74, 126
transmission, 19, 20, 21, 26, 28, 29, 30, 36, 39, 45
trans-tribal, 57, 67, 68, 108
Traore, Karim, ii
tribalism, 71, 84, 92, 132
Turkey, 55, 56
Tyler, 21, 45
Tylor, 11, 14, 20

U

Ugaas, 100, 102, 103, 104, 105, 106, 115
Ugaas Hassan, 105
Ugaas Wahays, 105
UNESCO, 11
Unites States, 56, 75
unity, 12, 14, 30, 37, 48, 54, 57, 58, 59, 60, 61, 65, 66, 76, 78, 80, 81, 84, 93, 98, 99, 103, 114, 116, 118, 129

USA. Voir Unites States

V

Van der Henst, 35

W

Wajeer, 57
Wanjiku Nyambura, 52
Watzlawick, 50, 78, 79
Weismann, 23, 45
western, vii, 14, 27, 58, 67, 69, 70, 71, 76, 77
White, 12, 44
Whitehead, 21, 45
Wiil Waal, 51
Wilber, 42, 50, 128
Wilson, viii, 18
Winnicottien, 24

X

xeer, 72, 94, 100, 101, 102, 103, 104, 105, 106, 107, 117, 119, 125, 128, 129
Xeer, 114, 115
xeer-dhaqameed, 48

Y

Yasiin C. Kenedid, 50

www.ingramcontent.com/pod-product-compliance
Lightning Source LLC
Chambersburg PA
CBHW070553170426
43201CB00012B/1828